CRYPTOCURRENCY
A Practical Guide To Investing In Six Cryptocurrencies

STACY JOSEPH

Cryptocurrency
Copyright © 2018 by Stacy Joseph

No part of this publication may be reproduced, distributed, or transmitted in any form or by any means, including photocopying, recording, or other electronic or mechanical methods, without the prior written permission of the author, except in the case of brief quotations embodied in critical reviews and certain other non-commercial uses permitted by copyright law.

Tellwell Talent
www.tellwell.ca

ISBN
978-1-77370-589-7 (Paperback)
978-1-77370-590-3 (eBook)

Table of Contents

Preface...v

Introduction......................................vii

Chapter 1: The History of Cryptocurrencies...........1
- The beginning 3
- Pre-Bitcoin virtual currencies...............................4
- The birth of Bitcoin...6
- The first experiment 11
- The Use of Cryptocurrencies in Crime 14
- Advantages of cryptocurrencies 16
- Disadvantages of cryptocurrencies...........................17
- References 19

Chapter 2: Bitcoin.............................21
- What is unique about the currency?......................... 23
- Bitcoin Wallets.. 25
- Why might people invest in Bitcoin?.........................27
- Challenges facing Bitcoin 28
- The future of Bitcoin 31
- References 35

Chapter 3: Litecoin............................37
- Litecoin vs other coins 40
- Litecoin Wallet.. 40
- Challenges facing Litecoin 43
- Why might people invest in Litecoin? 45
- The Future of Litecoin 46
- References 50

Chapter 4: Ethereum............................53
- How it works.. 55

- Why Ethereum is unique 57
- How to exchange Ethereum 59
- Ethereum Wallet 60
- Why might people invest in Ethereum? 61
- Challenges facing Ethereum 65
- Expected downfall 69
- Survival expectation of Ethereum 70
- References 72

Chapter 5: Augur 73
- The future of Augur 78
- Why might people invest in Augur? 81
- Challenges facing Augur 84
- References 86

Chapter 6: Ripple 87
- How it works 88
- The future of Ripple 91
- Investing in the currency 93
- Why might people invest in Ripple? 94
- Passive versus active investing 95
- Challenges facing Ripple 97
- References 101

Chapter 7: Dash 103
- Difference from other currencies 104
- How it works 105
- What makes it unique? 108
- Exchanges that allow Dash trading 109
- Dash Wallets 110
- Why might people invest in Dash? 114
- Challenges facing Dash 116
- Is there a risk of Dash collapsing? 117
- References 119

Chapter 8: Conclusion 121

Preface

During the 2008 financial crisis, we witnessed a global collapse in assets. We saw wealth simply evaporate due to investor panic. We watched as opportunities to make profitable investments came and left as we were frozen from fear of the unknown. Will the crash continue? Or have we hit rock-bottom and it is only up from here?

What simple tool were we missing? Other than money to take action, information! Had we been informed, like many successful investors, we would have bought low and sold high. The development and growth in cryptocurrencies is the next profitable opportunity piling up before our eyes.

Cryptocurrency: A Practical Guide to Investing in Six Cryptocurrencies covers six digital currencies and provides a strong foundation to develop your portfolio strategy. This book is meant to jumpstart your pursuit of knowledge on some of the most popular and widely used cryptocurrencies; Bitcoin, Litecoin, Ethereum, Augur, Ripple and Dash.

Catch the train before it leaves the station, all while using this book as a guide to your destination.

Introduction

Let me tell you a story. You've probably heard it before, but it's worth hearing again.

On 1 April 1976, three friends – Steve Jobs, Steve Wozniak and Ronald Wayne – incorporated a company called Apple Computer Inc. Wayne got a 10% stake in the company, and his role included providing administrative oversight, as well as providing 'adult supervision' to the two Steves who were, then, in their early 20s.

Twelve days after incorporation, Wayne decided to sell his equity in the company because, unlike the other two, he had assets that could be seized by creditors if the venture failed. So he played it safe. He took $800 in exchange for his 10% stake and $1,500 to forfeit all claims against Apple. The rest, as they say, is history.

Fast-forward 41 years later. If Wayne had kept his 10% stake, it would have been worth over $75.5 billion today. Ouch. Here's the thing though: as Wayne has said in several interviews over the years, he made the right decision *based on the information that was available to him at the time.* Who could have foretold that personal computers would become a thing? Much as you and I might be tempted to think that was a stupid mistake on Wayne's part, the truth is, many of us would probably have made the same decision based on the same set of information available at the time. But what does this have to do with cryptocurrencies?

Everything.

You see, just as information, or the absence of it, informed Wayne's decision, so too does knowledge about cryptocurrencies impact people's decisions today around this new form of currency. What are they? How do you get them? Are they of any value? Do they have a future? Should you get involved or just ignore them? People are seeking answers to questions like these and more, hoping to build their understanding so that they can decide what their approach to cryptocurrencies should be.

Initially considered a passing fad, cryptocurrencies have shown that they are here to stay; they are the new form of money quickly replacing their traditional counterpart as we know it. For those already actively using them, that's pretty cool. For those who are either just starting out and those who are still trying to wrap their heads around what cryptocurrencies are, the whole topic can be somewhat intimidating. It is for these people that I have written this book.

In it, I break down and simplify the whole concept of cryptocurrencies. I walk through six examples in order for the reader to develop their confidence discussing them, create a starting point from which to explore further and, most importantly, have an advantage that Wayne didn't have at the time: information.

Nothing in this book is intended as advice on whether or not to buy or invest in cryptocurrencies – that's your job. Your job entails gathering the information, assessing your own risk tolerance, and making an informed financial decision considering all factors. Some of the content is technical, but I've done my best to make it easy to understand. Bear in mind however, that one book cannot teach you everything you need to know about cryptocurrencies, especially since we all have different levels of technological know-how. And make no mistake, fully understanding cryptocurrencies requires some degree of technological knowledge and familiarity with the subject. So, even after completing this book, you will find that there are still some aspects you need to read up on. Thankfully, there's Google. But for the most part, the key elements that will provide a strong foundational understanding of cryptocurrencies have been broken down for you.

If you don't want to end up at the bottom rung of the economic and wealth ladder, it is important to continuously learn and stay abreast of the times. This book aims to help you do both when it comes to cryptocurrencies. It provides relevant information, because ultimately, information is the critical commodity you need in order to engage with cryptocurrencies, either as an investment or simply a medium of transaction. I hope you will find it useful as you explore the transition from physical to digital currencies in today's world.

Stacy Joseph

Toronto, October, 2017

Chapter 1:
The History of Cryptocurrencies

Bitcoin, Litecoin,

Ethereum, Dash;

Mining up the Cryptos,

That has since replaced my Cash

Remember that nursery rhyme from way back when we were little kids? No? Neither do I. I just made it up. But I do remember this one:

The king was in his counting house,

Counting out his money;

The queen was in the parlour,

Eating bread and honey.

Could there be a starker reminder of how the meaning of money has changed than the juxtaposition of these two rhymes? Think about it for a moment: there was a time when money meant gold coins – solid, shiny, and ohsobulky gold coins. Imagine having to lug around a pocketful of gold coins every time you needed to go shopping. No wonder the king needed a 'counting house' just to count his money! Luckily, it occurred to our forefathers that things didn't have to be that way, and so we moved to paper money.

Invented by the Chinese, paper money is lightweight, easier to carry around, and has enough space to tell people what they need to know. "Counterfeiters Will be Decapitated" proclaimed the very first paper money; "In God We Trust" declares its modern American equivalent. Paper money enjoyed a long and dominant reign, but as with all things in life, a competitor eventually arose: mobile payments.

With advances in technology, it was only a matter of time before money became electronic. The advent of electronic devices, online banking, and the like made it possible to make virtual payments without holding physical cash. While the world was still coming to terms with the virtualization of payment, boom! A new form of currency hits the scene: cryptocurrencies. Well, no, not quite. Cryptocurrencies were not a sudden occurrence. They've been a long time coming, just as the evolution of money took much longer than my very abridged history of money suggests.

Like most internet services, what started out as a very 'niche' idea has grown to the point where the use of cryptocurrencies has become more prevalent and mainstream. New cryptocurrencies are frequently being introduced and more people than previously thought possible have begun using them.

There are big differences between traditional currencies and cryptocurrencies, which confuses people. A cryptocurrency is a digital means of exchange created and used by private individuals or groups. Most are not regulated by state or national governments and are therefore considered an alternative means of financial exchange outside of the state's monetary policy.

Using advanced mathematics and computer engineering principles, developers built extremely complex code systems or cryptographic protocols that are virtually impossible to break. They use these protocols to encrypt sensitive data transfers as well as to secure their units of transfers. This makes it difficult to attribute fund flows and transactions to a particular user, thus masking their identities.

The beginning

Long before the world was even aware of the internet at all, an American named David Chaum was already working on a way to shield users from internet surveillance. In the 1980s, he invented a 'blinding' algorithm that allowed for secure and unalterable exchange of information between parties, and this remains central to today's webbased encryption systems and cryptocurrencies.

In the late 1980s, Chaum attempted to commercialize the concept of cryptocurrency – or 'blinded money' as it was referred to then – and consequently enlisted a handful of cryptocurrency enthusiasts. He relocated to the Netherlands and founded DigiCash as a for-profit company that produced units of currency based on his blinding algorithm. DigiCash had a monopoly on supply, as is the case with the monopoly of central banks on traditional currency. And, just as is the case with Bitcoin and other modern cryptocurrencies, DigiCash is decentralized where a third party is not required to store clients' funds.In the late 1990s, a well-established software engineer, Wei Dai, came up with b-money, a virtual currency architecture that included many of the basic attributes of today's cryptocurrencies, like decentralization and complex anonymity user protection. Unfortunately, b-money never saw the light of day as a means of exchange as it was likely far too ahead of its time.

Pre-Bitcoin virtual currencies

Following the use of DigiCash, people started investing in and conducting research into the use of other electronic mediums for financial transactions such as PayPal - an online traditional money service that facilitates receiving and sending payments from almost everywhere in the world. Other people started imitating the DigiCash currency and came up with currencies such as WebMoney in Russia and E-Gold in the United States – the dominant virtual currency in the late 1990s and 2000s. It was mainly used as a digital gold buying and selling platform, and was controlled by a Florida-based company of the same name. The users of E-Gold used to send their old coins, trinkets, and jewelry to warehouses owned by E-Gold and in return, received the equivalent amount of E-Gold units dominated in ounces of gold. After receiving these units of currency, users could then trade them with other customers, exchange the units for US dollars, or cash them out in exchange for physical gold.

The use of E-Gold was at its peak in the mid-2000s; millions of people held active accounts with the company which processed billions of dollars in transactions every year. However, due to the currency's poor security protocols, it became an easy target for scammers and hackers, which left customers vulnerable to financial loss in the case of a cyber-attack. During this period, most of the activities carried out using the currency were considered risky, and, since it had lax legal compliance policies, it became known for its use in small scale Ponzi schemes and money laundering operations. In particular, the activities of a website called Shadowcrew – a forum for criminals who traded stolen credit and debit card numbers – soon drew the attention of the US Secret Service which launched an undercover operation. They soon discovered that EGold was among the carders' preferred money-transfer methods, because it allowed users to anonymously open accounts and transfer funds anywhere in the world. The platform began to face legal pressure and stopped operating in 2009, at which point a new digital currency was introduced: Bitcoin.

The birth of Bitcoin

Most people regard Bitcoin as the first modern cryptocurrency designed to serve in operations that required user anonymity, record-keeping through a blockchain, decentralized control, and built-in scarcity. At this point, we need a pit stop to define some of the terms that will be coming up repeatedly.

1. **Mining** is one of the unique technologies through which cryptocurrencies run. It is the process of adding transaction records to a cryptocurrency's public ledger of past transactions. Quite literally, mining is like digging into the algorithm of a network for Bitcoin or another cryptocurrency. Here's how it works: miners make use of computers to solve mathematical problems (algorithms, not arithmetic). These algorithms, when solved, cause more of the cryptocurrency to be added to the network and the miners get a reward for their trouble. The key purpose of the service is to perform a verification process that ensures that transactions are consistent, complete and cannot be altered.

2. **Blocks** are files where data related to a cryptocurrency's network is permanently recorded. A block

records the most recent transactions that have not yet entered any prior blocks. Thus, a block is like a page of a ledger.

3. A **blockchain** is a cryptocurrency's ledger of past transactions that serves to confirm transactions to the rest of the network as having taken place. It is called the blockchain because, well, it is a chain of blocks; each block is created using a special algorithm linking each blockchain to the next. Miners solve the algorithms by finding a hash (a cryptologic puzzle) that connects the new block with the old block.   Thus, a blockchain is an endless collection of blocks linked using cryptography.

I will expand on the meanings of these terms and discuss them in greater detail throughout the book. Now let's get back to where we left off.

Although Bitcoin came into play in 2009, it was first outlined in 2008 by Satoshi Nakamoto, the pseudonym for the person or group that introduced the currency.

Bitcoin was first released on 9 January 2009 in the form of Bitcoin 0.1. Enthusiastic supporters of the digital currency started mining and exchanging the currency. Only Windows 2000, Windows XP and Windows NT could support Bitcoin 0.1.0 to 0.1.5 releases. Immediately after releasing the first version of Bitcoin to the public, Nakamoto went on to correct the different node and network communication errors that existed in the release and also worked with several associates on improving the usability for clients. For instance, the following version prevented someone from entering their own address in the address book and also included text to explain transaction details for coins that were generated.

Almost a year after the introduction of Bitcoin to the public, Bitcoin 0.2 was released in December 2009 and it accommodated the Linux Operating System (OS). The community at this time had become active participants in the currency's development. In addition to that, the new release had the ability to utilize multiple processors in the generation of blocks. Before this release, one could only use one thread, however, with the new release, having a duo or quad core would double or quadruple the production respectively. Another major leap was the creation of JSON RPC API, a lightweight data-interchange format that can represent numbers, strings, ordered sequences of values, and collections of name/value pairs which enabled third party services to communicate with the network and the blockchain.

At this time, only a small group who were part of the early developers knew about Bitcoin. In November 2009, a forum was created on Bitcoin.org and acted as the precursor for today's Bitcoin Talk. This forum took the popularity of the currency to greater heights. As the online community grew, ideas were swiftly conceptualized and implemented by numerous teams throughout various releases.

With this increased public engagement, the currency began to not only receive praises, but also criticism for various flaws found when the operating principles of Bitcoin were analysed. At the same time, the concept of transaction fees was recognized and individuals began discussing the idea of Bitcoin being traceable. Another version of Bitcoin, 0.3, was introduced in July 2010 despite the growth in the number of people using the currency. This development caused a problem concerning mining; it became increasingly difficult even though it was possible to use a computer's graphic processor's computational abilities to mine. A mere two weeks after the release, ArtForz, a legendary figure in the crypto community, shook things up. ArtForz is said to have abruptly appeared out of nowhere and simultaneously possessed an incredible amount of hands-on knowledge about how to tweak mining hardware performance. He came on the scene and was able to generate his Bitcoin block within six days, an impressive achievement.

On 6 August 2010, a major vulnerability was discovered in the Bitcoin protocol. The verification of transactions was not completed properly before inclusion it in the blockchain. This problem led to users bypassing the economic restriction placed on Bitcoin. The problem engendered by such a bypass was obvious – users would be able to create indefinite numbers of Bitcoin. A few noticed the flaw and on 15 August, the vulnerability was exploited. 184 *billion* Bitcoin were generated in a transaction and sent to two addresses that existed in the network! Several hours after the transactions, the transfers were noted and deleted from the blockchain. This was done only after fixing and forking the network to an updated version of the Bitcoin protocol. **Forking** refers to the splitting of source code into different development directions, meaning that a distinct version of a program is developed. In the history of Bitcoin, this was the only major security flaw that has been found and exploited.

As time went by, miners competed to have a share of the limited supply of blocks. It soon dawned on miners that they could work for months and go unrewarded for their efforts, which discouraged many. Soon though, they came up with an idea to solve the variance in their income. The solution they found was **pooled mining**, a mining approach where multiple clients contribute to the generation of a block, and then split the block reward according to the contributed processing power.

On 27 November 2010, Slush's pool, which was the name of the first Bitcoin Pooled Mining (BPM), came into existence. The pooled mining operated on the strategy of sharing the incomes but the method has been found to be vulnerable to cheating. With time, the idea of mining as a group has evolved even though the strategy remains the same. In December of the same year, a user known as *doublec* compiled Bitcoin meant for the Nokia N900 mobile computer and the very next day, he received 0.42 Bitcoin that was sent to him by a user known as *ribuck*. This was the first peertopeer Bitcoin transaction to be registered.

The first experiment

At the end of 2010, Nakamoto released his/her/their final version of the currency, Bitcoin 0.3.9, and decided to leave the project completely. The departure of the creator of Bitcoin did not have a considerable impact on the circulation and development of the currency, since the community wilfully accepted these responsibilities. In order to improve the efficiency in communications within the Bitcoin community, the Bitcoin Improvement Proposal (BIP) was introduced. Since Bitcoin has no formal governance structure, this became the standard method of communicating the different ideas being generated.

By this time, many ideas started to emerge on the different ways people could improve Bitcoin. However, not all those ideas could be implemented in the different upgrades, so people began conducting their own individual projects. The first idea that was integrated in the Bitcoin upgrade was the one that required binding Bitcoin to DNS (domain name system) servers. This idea led to the development of the Namecoin. Following this development, developers began experimenting with maturity, block reward, block time, and other parameters of the currency which resulted in the creation of currencies like SolidCoin, GeistGeld, and iXcoin among others.

As mentioned earlier, with the release of each new version, mining had become more difficult. With the increased difficulty in mining Bitcoin, people started migrating to the use of GPU and FPGA farms. (The GPU, or graphics processing unit, is a part of the video rendering system of a computer. It renders 3D graphics and visual effects so that the CPU (central processing unit) doesn't have to do that. The CPU instead focuses on its job of executing the software loaded on the computer. FPGA, on the other hand, are reconfigurable circuits which, like Lego blocks, can be put together to form different objects, i.e. they can be used to build almost any digital circuit).

The public was also concerned about the errors that were present in SHA256, the cryptographic algorithm that creates imprints of messages. (SHAs are used in various applications related to information security). In response, developers and individuals started carrying out experiments that could correct the flaws. The first coin that abandoned the SHA256 was a cryptocurrency called Tenebrix, which had a solid GPU resistance. The currency was developed on an algorithm that appeared as a password-gen function, although it never became well known to the public. Litecoin was the next cryptocurrency to be introduced, and it was welcomed enthusiastically by the cryptocurrency community. Litecoin is to Bitcoin what silver is to gold. People embraced it much better than they did Tenebrix, which had a pre-mine. (A pre-mine is where a developer allocates a certain amount of currency credit to a particular address before releasing the source code to the open community, a practice considered unfair by some). Litecoin led to the abandonment of the GPU being used for mining the more expensive Bitcoin, and enabled people to start using the CPU.

A new principle known as the proof-of-stake was introduced in the summer of 2011 in an effort to fight against the unequal distribution of voting power. With this principle, the acceptance of an individual's vote was to be accepted based on the number of Bitcoin a stakeholder owns and was to be proven using one's private keys. This was different from the earlier principle where a person's vote was accepted based on his transaction history, and that could be proven by the share of computing resources one could make available in the network. One year after this new principle took off, Peercoin was introduced, a hybrid that utilized both the proofofstake and proofofwork principles.

In the period between 2011 and 2012, there were several rapid developments in the world of cryptocurrencies, including its expansion into the mobile world. Bitcoin mobile, the first Bitcoin app made for iPad, was developed in July 2011 by Intervex Digital. In August 2011, the first P2Pool decentralized pool was introduced, in addition to a serious analysis of the anonymity that existed in the Bitcoin system. The first Bitcoin laundry was conducted by Mike Gogulski. It is also in 2011 that Ripple, another cryptocurrency, was accepted by the community. Ripple had initially been introduced in 2004 in the digital currency market by Ryan Fugger, a developer based in Vancouver. He started building it in 2005 as a financial service that could provide safe payments to members of the digital currency community through a worldwide network. Individuals began realizing that the currency could act as a means of financial exchange that would solve the discrepancies that were present in cryptocurrencies.

In that same year, Jed McCaleb started working on a digital currency system that could aid in the verification of transactions through consensus among members of the network, instead of using the mining process associated with Bitcoin. Another significant development at the end of that year was when Alan Reiner released BIP 0010 Multi-signature Transaction Distribution (multi-sig), meaning that more than one key was needed to authorize a Bitcoin transaction. This proposal was implemented and tried in the older versions of Bitcoin software that was used in signing transactions in the offline-wallet. The multi-sigs were introduced to Bitcoin system on 30 March 2012.

The Use of Cryptocurrencies in Crime

It was a major operation by the FBI and breathless news coverage by multiple news channels that first brought the name 'Bitcoin' to the consciousness of most people around the world. They had probably heard it now and again, but I don't think I would be far off the mark if I said few people actually knew what it was. Along with Bitcoin, another name entered our collective consciousness following that FBI operation: Silk Road.

Silk Road was the shadowy, illegal drug trading platform hidden deep within the belly of the dark web, kept out of the public eye through the use of the anonymizing tool *Tor*. It was launched in February 2011 and it thrived primarily because the anonymity of the dark web served as a protective shield for the identities of buyers, sellers, and the site's administrators. Payments were made in Bitcoin because it was virtually untraceable. It is believed that billions of dollars in transactions were conducted in Bitcoin through this site. Over $34 million dollars in Bitcoin was seized in the raid against the pseudonymous Dread Pirate Roberts, the mastermind behind Silk Road. This was said to be his commission from the illegal trading. Dread Pirate Roberts was later found to be a 29-year-old former University of Texas physics student named Ross Ulbricht. Thus, when the FBI brought down Silk Road, Bitcoin was inevitably drawn into the fight. Ulbricht's trial for narcotics and money laundering offences was as much about the status of Bitcoin as a currency as it was about the illegality of Ulbricht's actions. He was later found guilty and is currently serving a life term in jail with no option of parole.

Unsurprisingly, given how lucrative a business it had been, there have been several other attempts to reopen Silk Road, with the FBI continuing to shut them down. Most recently, AlphaBay, the *de facto* successor to Silk Road, made the news when it was shut down in July 2017. Started in 2014, it was ten times bigger than Silk Road by the time it was shut down, with over 400,000 users and between $600,000 and $800,000 in transactions *per day*. Most of that was in Bitcoin, but the site also accepted Ethereum, another cryptocurrency we'll be exploring later.

With the wide publicity generated by these cases, it is no wonder why people who don't understand cryptocurrencies still associate them with illegal activities. But as the rest of this book will show, these currencies have become more mainstream and have acquired legitimacy within the world of legitimate businesses.

Advantages of cryptocurrencies

Cost Saving: One of the benefits to cryptocurrencies is that there is no transaction fee required for an exchange. At the moment, miners are usually paid by the network for their work and therefore users are not charged any fee. The only fee that may arise in the use of cryptocurrencies is the engagement with third-party services such as Coinbase, which create and maintain their Bitcoin wallets where users can store their cryptocurrencies before use. Such wallets act in a similar way to PayPal by storing the currencies, and they may charge a small fee.

Built-in Scarcity: Many of the current cryptocurrencies are created in such a way that they are scarce. The source code from which these cryptocurrencies are created limits the number of units that can exist at any one time. This makes the cryptocurrencies precious due to their scarcity, something uncommon in conventional currencies. The scarcity also helps protect the currency from inflation and therefore ensuring its value.

Immediate Settlement: with the purchase of real property, several third parties are usually involved which may result in the payment of fees and delays. The use of cryptocurrency blockchains can be compared to a large property rights database where contracts can be enforced or formulated in a way that excludes a third party's approval. This usually takes only a fraction of the time and expenses required by traditional asset transfer methods.

Prevention of Identity Theft: When people use credit cards to purchase commodities from a trader, they are usually compelled to give them the complete credit line even in cases of small purchases. These credit cards operate on the pull principle where the store pulls the needed amount from the account. As opposed to cryptocurrencies that use the push mechanism, whereby the buyer only sends the amount they want to the trader without giving up any additional information. This protects users from identity theft.

Decrease in Barriers and Costs for International Transactions: Cryptocurrencies do not have any regional boundaries like traditional currencies do. This helps eliminate the various barriers and costs that may exist in international transfers. Users are able to transfer to any recipient anywhere in the world free of charge. This is a great advantage considering that traditional currencies can charge fees totaling up to 15% of the amount sent. With the cost saving aspect of cryptocurrencies, they are considered the way of the future.

Disadvantages of cryptocurrencies

Lack of regulation: One of the biggest disadvantages associated with the use of cryptocurrencies is its use in illegal activities as they are not easily traceable. Bitcoin, for instance, was the main currency that was used in the purchase of illegal drugs on Silk Road and on AlphaBay before they were shut down.

Tax evasion: The use of cryptocurrencies has been attracting many tax evaders especially in countries where even the people using cryptocurrencies are required by the law to pay taxes, such as in the United States. Due to the ability of people to use fake names online, some use names other than the ones registered on their W-2 (IRS tax form), therefore making it possible for them to evade taxes. Opponents of cryptocurrencies argue that its use will lead to increased tax evasion which will in turn lead to a lag in a country's economy.

With our general understanding of the history of cryptocurrencies, Bitcoin, Litecoin, Ethereum, Augur, Ripple and Dash will be examined further in the chapters that follow.

References

Australian Associated Press. (2014, April 10). Bitcoin firms dumped by National Australia Bank as "too risky." Retrieved from The Guardian website: https://www.theguardian.com/world/2014/apr/10/bitcoin-dumped-by-national-australia-bank-as-too-risky

Bitcoinweb Hosting. (2017). History of Bitcoin. Retrieved from Bitcoinweb Hosting: http://historyofbitcoin.org/

Bitcoin Wiki, Pooled Mining. Retrieved from https://en.bitcoin.it/wiki/Pooled_mining

Chavez-Dreyfuss, G., & Connor, M. (2014, August 28). Bitcoin shows staying power as online merchants chase digital sparkle. Retrieved from Reuters website:

https://www.reuters.com/article/2014/08/28/us-usa-bitcoin-retailers-analysis-idUSKBN0GS0AG20140828

Clarke, J. B. (2015, October 15). Provisions: Privacy Preserving proof of solvency for Bitcoin exchange. Retrieved from International Association for Cryptologic Research: https://eprint.iacr.org/2015/1008.pdf

CNN tech (2017). What is Bitcoin. Retrieved from CNN website: http://money.cnn.com/infographic/technology/what-is-bitcoin/

Dougherty, C. (2013, December 05). Bankers Balking at Bitcoin in U.S. as Real-World Obstacles Mount. Retrieved from Bloomberg Website: https://www.bloomberg.com/news/2013-12-05/bitcoin-skepticism-by-bankers-from-china-to-u-s-hinders-growth.html

Durden, T. (2017, June 23). Is Bitcoin Money? Retrieved from Zero Hedge Website: www.zerohedge.com/news/2017-06-22/bitcoin-money

Griffith, K. (2014, April 16). A Quick History of Cryptocurrencies BBTC — Before Bitcoin. Retrieved from bitcoinmagazine.com: https://bitcoinmagazine.com/articles/quick-history-cryptocurrencies-bbtc-bitcoin-1397682630/

Hill, K. (2013, December 05). Bitcoin Valued At $1300 By Bank of America Analysts. Retrieved from Forbes' website: http://www.forbes.com/sites/kashmirhill/2013/12/05/bank-of-america-analysts-say-Bitcoin-value-is-1300/

Knight, W. (2017, April 18). The Technology Behind Bitcoin Is Shaking Up Much More Than Money. Retrieved from MIT Technology Review: https://www.technologyreview.com/s/604148/the-technology-behind-bitcoin-is-shaking-up-much-more-than-money/

Martucci, B. (2016). What Is Cryptocurrency – How It Works, History & Bitcoin Alternatives. Retrieved from moneycrashers.com: http://www.moneycrashers.com/cryptocurrency-history-bitcoin-alternatives/

Pita, P. (2017, May 15). Cryptocurrency – Pros and Cons of Each. Retrieved from Virtual Reality Times: http://virtualrealitytimes.com/2017/05/15/cryptocurrency-pros-and-cons-of-each/

Rosic, A. (2016, June 28). 5 Benefits of Cryptocurrency: A New Economy For The Future. Retrieved from decentralize.today: https://decentralize.today/5-benefits-of-cryptocurrency-a-new-economy-for-the-future-925747434103

Sparkes M. (March 2015) US auctions 50,000 Bitcoin seized from Silk Road. Retrieved from http://www.telegraph.co.uk/technology/news/11451379/US-auctions-50000-Bitcoin-seized-from-Silk-Road.html

Chapter 2: Bitcoin

It is a transaction that will probably be forever known as one of the, *ahem!* notsosmart moves of the century. In May 2010, a programmer named Laslo Hanyecz, who was a member of the Bitcoin discussion forum, offered 10,000 bitcoins in exchange for someone to order him a pizza at Papa John's. That number of bitcoins is today valued at over $6 million! That's some pretty expensive pizza right there. We can't blame Laslo though. At the time of the transaction, that number of bitcoins was worth US$25. But imagine if he had kept all those bitcoins! He could've been buying pizzas for his friends every day for the rest of his life. The Bitcoin community commemorates that transaction on 22 May of every year as Bitcoin Pizza Day. That story shows the tremendous growth in value that has happened to Bitcoin. But how did it get to that? How did it become so popular? Let's backtrack a little.

Of all the cryptocurrencies out there, Bitcoin is, without doubt, the most popular. It has gained notoriety since its creation in 2009, and is now known all over the world, even if most people don't know how to mine it, use it or profit from it. As previously mentioned, the true identity of the creator of Bitcoin is yet to be revealed, but it's creator went by the pseudonym Satoshi Nakamoto. The creation of Bitcoin followed ideas contained in a white paper written by Nakamoto. Titled *"Bitcoin; A peer to peer electronic cash system,"* it was released on 31 October 2008 in what was known as the Cryptography Mailing List. Following this idea, an open source code was created and was revealed to the public in January 2009. In the same year, the first block of Bitcoin was released and nicknamed 'Genesis.' This step allowed the first mining process of Bitcoin to take place. In the same month, the first Bitcoin transaction took place between the creator of Bitcoin and a certain Hal Finney, who was later identified as a developer and a cryptography activist.

As a reward for downloading the application on which Bitcoin operated, Finney received 10 bitcoins. After the mine of the first block, which was valued at 50 bitcoins, the popularity of Bitcoin began to grow. It has been argued that its creator, Nakamoto, was able to mine close to 1 million bitcoins before ceasing to be involved with the currency. Gavin Andersen took over the administration of Bitcoin and became the first developer of the Bitcoin Foundation.

In October 2009, the Bitcoin currency was valued in the same way as previous traditional currencies. The valuation created the new liberty standards which placed the value of one dollar at 1,309 bitcoins. The value of the first common Bitcoin transaction was subject to negotiation on some of the forums dealing with Bitcoin issues.

What is unique about the currency?

Remember blockchain? Here's more information about it. As noted earlier, a blockchain is a form of public ledger that is used in the recording of all the Bitcoin transactions that take place. This technology has been recognized for its ability to overcome some of the major challenges faced in the conduct of transactions in society. The main idea behind the operation of blockchain technology is that it does not require a central regulator, and various agreements can be established without a third-party regulator. The computer network is made up of communicating nodes that allow the running of the Bitcoin Network. These nodes are the basis of Bitcoin transactions. Like traditional money, which has a central depository unit, this technology enables the broadcasting of all Bitcoin transactions. The nodes allow for easy validation and verification by creating a ledger of all transactions that are carried out. The maintenance of the ledger is also done by the communication nodes. The computations that are carried out allow the generation of more Bitcoin to be used in future transactions.

Blockchain technology is being applied in many areas today. For example, the diamond industry is currently adopting the use of blockchain technology with the aim of distinguishing the legitimacy of the sources of diamonds in order to avoid conflict diamonds and fraudulent diamond transactions. Careful examination of the blockchain data provided allows the identification of diamond transactions that are fraudulent. Carbon trading deals and the security of digital health records are other areas eyeing the use of blockchain technology.

Blockchain technology faces a challenge due to its complex nature and the questions which have been raised around its security. The Hyperledger, an opensource collaborative effort created to advance cross-industry blockchain technologies, has been introduced by the Linux foundation to address some of these concerns.

To guarantee the security of Bitcoin, the system has a proofofwork network which requires miners to be able to identify a special key number. The identification of this number is a long, hectic process that requires a lot of input not only of resources but also of time. This therefore means that the programmers who perform data mining have to go through lots of procedures to get the special key and gain the reward. The chaining block and the proofofwork system make it very challenging for anybody to try and modify Bitcoin.

In the recent past, there has been infighting in the Bitcoin community in a bid to gain central control in trading, and especially around the issue of moving money quickly and cheaply. As a result, the Bitcoin community split into two factions, each in favor of two different and "mutually incompatible solutions while accusing each other of incompetence, conspiracy, self-aggrandizement, and generally being the devil." The fights that have arisen have greatly undermined the currency and increased its volatility.

On 1 August 2017, the currency split into Bitcoin and Bitcoin Cash, an alternative cryptocurrency, in a chain split that had been anticipated for months. The split, called a 'hard fork,' saw the creators releasing completely new software that allows for eight times the number of transactions per block, meaning Bitcoin Cash can process transactions faster. Anyone who owns Bitcoin will also own the same number of Bitcoin Cash units. However, Bitcoin Cash is not worth the same as Bitcoin. As of this writing, a unit of Bitcoin Cash is valued around US$540, while one Bitcoin is worth more than US$4,300.

Bitcoin Wallets

A digital wallet system is applied with regards to the storage of Bitcoin. The main purpose of the wallet is to store the necessary information with which a person can transact in the currency. The creation of the wallet was a means of ensuring a user-friendly environment. This is because, although Bitcoin can be stored and held in wallets, they are basically inseparable from the blockchain ledger. Thus, the wallet stores the digital credentials for an individual's Bitcoin holdings and allows him or her to access them and spend them as required, all the while still remaining part of the blockchain. The use of the wallet has created a unique technology that allows the use of the public key cryptography. This means that the encryption system holds two main keys, one which is public and the other private. The wallet is accessed by having these two main key systems.

The main types of wallets are software and online. Software wallets were created with the aim of connecting to the network and promoting the ability to spend Bitcoin. Software wallets are divided into two main categories that enable access to the currency for spending, namely full clients and lightweight clients.

Online wallets have a somewhat similar functionality as software wallets, but are easier to use. With online wallets, credentials are stored online unlike the software wallet, which is mainly stored on the hardware of the Bitcoin technology network. Online wallets are based purely on trust in the wallet service provider. If the security of the online storage service provider is breached, well, you could lose a large amount of Bitcoin and, coincidently, money. Mt. Gox, which was previously one of the largest exchangers of Bitcoin, faced such a breach in 2011.

Described as a towering example of renegade entrepreneurism, Tokyo-based Mt. Gox dominated the field of Bitcoin exchange. In 2014, it filed for bankruptcy after it was hacked. In total, it lost US$460 million dollars of people's money. Although it was later found that the company itself was poorly managed and beset by inexperience, Mt. Gox is a cautionary tale of what could happen to *any* company.

I should point out that wallets can also be physical in nature, allowing users to spend Bitcoin offline. Physical wallets hold a physical Bitcoin, which works as a bearer instrument that can be used to store Bitcoin more safely or for trade offline. A physical bitcoin holds the coin's public address and a hidden private key. Sometimes, physical wallets have credentials which are printed on the metal.

Why might people invest in Bitcoin?

Bitcoin has recently been adopted as a form of investment. Investors purchased Bitcoin as protection from increased rates of inflation. The most notable event of all time was during the financial crisis in Cyprus in 2012 and 2013. The purchase of Bitcoin increased dramatically as people feared that their savings accounts could be confiscated.

Bitcoin funds is another way through which people are making investment in Bitcoin; if you're rich, you could also become a Bitcoin venture capitalist. One of the better-known names to have gone this route is Peter Thiel, one of the founders and former CEO of PayPal who, in 2002, took the company public. He and some of his associates invested US$3 million in Bitpay, funding the Bitcoin infrastructure, including the creation of companies that are service providers in the Bitcoin sector.

Like most currencies and even products in the market, the value of Bitcoin has fluctuated since it was created.

This volatility has mainly been associated with economic changes and the questions which have sometimes been raised about the security of Bitcoin. In 2016, the *Wall Street Journal* reported that the price of Bitcoin was becoming more stable than that of gold. By 2017, the price of one Bitcoin had surpassed the price of one ounce of gold, and now worth thrice its value. Looking at the growth of the market in the recent past, and assuming this trend was to continue (big assumption); it wouldn't be a bad move to adopt this form of investment to diversify your portfolio. Remember the US$6 million pizza? It seems investment in Bitcoin works best if the currency is bought and held for a few years. Day trading Bitcoin, as is often done with stocks and other investments may not be a beneficial strategy. Extreme swings in volatility can potentially lead to the realization of large losses, and the use of margin trading accounts simply amplifies this risk.

In a CNN article referenced at the end of this chapter on why people should acquire Bitcoin, the ability to remain anonymous through Bitcoin's technology was put forward as a big factor that will continue to increase its popularity and usage. It was argued that the combination of factors like being able to buy merchandise anonymously as well as making international payments easily and cheaply with Bitcoin contribute to the currency's outlook.

Challenges facing Bitcoin

In August 2010, the vulnerability of Bitcoin was laid bare after some people were able to go against Bitcoin protocol, allowing them to get Bitcoin without going through the verification process as they normally would. In this period, about 184 Billion Bitcoin were created and they were passed to two major addresses which existed on the Bitcoin network. Although the Bitcoin team was able to successfully erase the transaction from the networks and able to create a regulatory platform following this breach, the fact that it happened at all illustrates that security vulnerability should never be discounted.

Then there is the rather obscure nature of the currency – although guaranteeing anonymity is one of its main strengths, it is also one of its challenges. If Bitcoin is stolen, its recovery is virtually impossible because you cannot find the person who has it. That lesson was forcefully brought home to a hapless Bloomberg reporter in 2013. TV anchor Matt Miller was doing a segment on *12 Days of Bitcoin* when he flashed his Bitcoin paper wallet on TV, inadvertently showing the corresponding QR code on the paper wallet for his private Bitcoin address. A viewer quickly scanned the code and promptly stole the $20 value of the coin.

One of the challenges facing the growth of Bitcoin is the refusal of banks to associate with people and companies that use it as a form of payment. Could it be because they fear competition? Not according to the banks. Their primary reservation, they argue, is that companies using Bitcoin have generally been associated with some form of criminal activity. Banks say they look at the idea behind cryptocurrencies as very progressive but because it lacks the traditional qualities or definitions of currency, they tend to stay away from it. National Bank of Australia, for instance, closed the accounts of all the companies associated with Bitcoin in 2014.

Another potential threat to the progress of Bitcoin as a currency is the fact that many people are worried about the preservation of the currency. This is mainly attributed to the volatility of Bitcoin and the increasing difficulty in predicting its movements. It doesn't help matters when a well-respected magazine like Forbes declares that the cryptocurrency is a bubble which is about to burst. The magazine has argued in the recent past that the concept of Bitcoin was created to benefit a few people. Other magazines, journals, and opinion leaders have echoed similar sentiments. For readers of these magazines, that is just one more reason not to make any direct investments in Bitcoin or cryptocurrencies in general.

Perhaps the most critical of all is its legal classification. Bitcoin has attained some of the major characteristics to be called money; however, this qualification continues to be disputed by many. National laws on the recognition of money and what constitutes legal tender have yet to uniformly agree. While some countries have explicitly allowed its use and trade, others have banned or restricted it. In the US for instance, the Treasury Department classified Bitcoin as a convertible decentralized virtual currency in 2013, and the IRS taxes it as property. Bitcoin's meets the characterization as money but not as legal tender poses a major threat to the currency.

In New York City, an individual was taken to court over allegations that he had carried out money laundering using Bitcoin. The district judge ruled that he did not have any jurisdiction because Bitcoin was not money, but the federal judge agreed that if Bitcoin met all the qualifications of money and especially the fact that it was a store of value, then it was money. This uncertainty and lack of clarity around its classification therefore poses a challenge to potential adopters.

Finally, another major threat to Bitcoin is that it has been adopted as a form of payment for criminal activities, as we saw with Silk Road and AlphaBay. This has attracted the attention of not only financial regulators but also of law enforcement authorities and legislative bodies. This is a threat to investing in Bitcoin as investors fear the whole thing could be shut down. The Securities and Exchange Commission (SEC) in the United States gave directives against the use of the virtual currency when making investments. The United States Senate also held a hearing in November 2013 on the use of the modern form of the virtual currency.

The future of Bitcoin

The future of the Bitcoin currency lies in the economics of Bitcoin. As discussed above, although Bitcoin has been classified as a form of digital currency, there continues to be many arguments as to whether Bitcoin is a form of money or not. According to economists, Bitcoin can be classified as money because of its ability to store value, to be used as a medium of exchange, and to be a unit of account. The most important factor to remember is that Bitcoin is able to serve as a medium of exchange; this being the definition of money in its truest form. Bitcoin should therefore be classified as money by anyone questioning its validity. According to recent media reports, over 200,000 merchants around the world today now accept Bitcoin. The number of merchants has grown incredibly from the 2015 statistics, when the number of merchants accepting Bitcoin was at 100,000. This growth is attributed to a reduction in fees. Merchants only pay a fee between 0 and 2% whereas credit card processors charge fees between 2% and 3%. Major institutions and elite individuals are beginning to accept Bitcoin as a form of payment. Political candidates like Jeff Kurzon have accepted donations made in Bitcoin. The University of Nicosia in Cyprus took the first step in accepting Bitcoin as a form of payment for tuition. Additionally, the University started offering a degree in the study of the digital currencies.

Among other adopters of the currency as a form of payment are many healthcare providers, which now accept Bitcoin. The *My Doctor Medical Group* and the *RapidMed Urgent Care Center* in Lewisville, Texas are some of the service providers known to have adopted Bitcoin as a form of payment. Many other medical providers have expressed interest in using Bitcoin as a method of payment. With many people in the world continually taking up the use of the currency, it is most likely that the use of Bitcoin will only continue to grow stronger.

Inevitably, businesses looking to tap into the success of the currency have increased. With the growth in its popularity and user base, many service providers have come up to provide a platform through which online payments can be made, allowing merchants to make and accept payments. Some examples of Bitcoin payment service providers include Bitpay or the Coinbase system. Furthermore, the growth of online service providers has been facilitated by the ability to convert Bitcoin into local currencies such as US dollars or British pounds. The merchants who accept this form of payment convert Bitcoin into local currency through service providers, who then charge a service fee for the conversion from one form to the other.

Based only on its continuing acceptance into the mainstream, I would say that Bitcoin has a bright future. There are, of course, no guarantees. There's no telling what a possible split due to the rift earlier mentioned, or even other factors, may do to the currency over the long term.

As mentioned earlier, one of the threats facing Bitcoin is the lack of collaboration from financial institutions like banks. They have opted to stay out of the Bitcoin business, insisting that the currency cannot be adopted in the same way as traditional forms of currency. One example is the closure by the National Bank of Australia of the accounts of companies and people using Bitcoin as a form of payment.

Whereas some banks believe in the ability of Bitcoin to become a success in the ecommerce sector, many banks have argued that it poses a serious threat to traditional money and money transfer providers. To curb this belief however, some investors have created banks like the Bitcoin Crypto Bank that allow the deposits in Bitcoin currency without having to pay any fees.

These factors, in combination with those mentioned under 'challenges' above, are what investors will consider before deciding to invest. But while there are many factors challenging the progress of Bitcoin, its collapse does not appear to be imminent and its growth appears to be prominent

References

Australian Associated Press. (2014, April 10). Bitcoin firms dumped by National Australia Bank as "too risky." Retrieved from The Guardian website: https://www.theguardian.com/world/2014/apr/10/bitcoin-dumped-by-national-australia-bank-as-too-risky

Bitcoinweb hosting. (2017). History of Bitcoin. Retrieved from Bitcoinweb hosting: http://historyofbitcoin.org/

Chavez-Dreyfuss, G., & Connor, M. (2014, August 28). Bitcoin shows staying power as online merchants chase digital sparkle. Retrieved from Reuters website: https://www.reuters.com/article/2014/08/28/us-usa-bitcoin-retailers-analysis-idUSKBN0GS0AG20140828

Clarke, J. B. (2015, October 15). Provisions: Privacy Preserving proof of solvency for Bitcoin exchange. Retrieved from International Association for Cryptologic Research: https://eprint.iacr.org/2015/1008.pdf

CNN tech (2017). What is Bitcoin. Retrieved from CNN website: http://money.cnn.com/infographic/technology/what-is-bitcoin/

Dougherty, C. (2013, December 05). Bankers Balking at Bitcoin in U.S. as Real-World Obstacles Mount. Retrieved from Bloomberg Website: https://www.bloomberg.com/news/2013-12-05/bitcoin-skepticism-by-bankers-from-china-to-u-s-hinders-growth.html

Durden, T. (2017, June 23). Is Bitcoin Money? Retrieved from Zero Hedge Website: www.zerohedge.com/news/2017-06-22/bitcoin-money

Griffith, K. (2014, April 16). A Quick History of Cryptocurrencies BBTC — Before Bitcoin. Retrieved from bitcoinmagazine.com: https://bitcoinmagazine.com/articles/quick-history-cryptocurrencies-bbtc-bitcoin-1397682630/

Hill, K. (2013, December 05). Bitcoin Valued At $1300 By Bank of America Analysts. Retrieved from Forbes.com website: http://www.forbes.com/sites/kashmirhill/2013/12/05/bank-of-america-analysts-say-Bitcoin-value-is-1300/

Knight, W. (2017, April 18). The Technology Behind Bitcoin Is Shaking Up Much More Than Money. Retrieved from MIT Technology Review:

https://www.technologyreview.com/s/604148/the-technology-behind-bitcoin-is-shaking-up-much-more-than-money/

Martucci, B. (2016). What Is Cryptocurrency – How It Works, History & Bitcoin Alternatives. Retrieved from moneycrashers.com: http://www.moneycrashers.com/cryptocurrency-history-bitcoin-alternatives/

Pita, P. (2017, May 15). Cryptocurrency – Pros and Cons of Each. Retrieved from virtualrealitytimes.com: http://virtualrealitytimes.com/2017/05/15/cryptocurrency-pros-and-cons-of-each/

Rosic, A. (2016, June 28). 5 Benefits of Cryptocurrency: A New Economy For The Future. Retrieved from decentralize.today: https://decentralize.today/5-benefits-of-cryptocurrency-a-new-economy-for-the-future-925747434103

Smith, J (August 2017) The Bitcoin Cash Hard Fork Will Show Us Which Coin Is Best. http://fortune.com/2017/08/11/bitcoin-cash-hard-fork-price-date-why/

Chapter 3: Litecoin

Hands up if, like me, you think the name "Litecoin" is better suited to a Marvel comic superhero than a currency. Still, I'd take it over the very nerdy-sounding Ethereum, anyday. So Litecoin. Where did it come from?

In the beginning... A former Google employee named Charlie Lee released his creation, the Litecoin, on GitHub. Litecoin was basically a slightly modified Bitcoin. As with all the other digital currencies, Litecoin enabled (and still enables) peer-to-peer transactions without third party involvement on an open-source, decentralised global payment network, same as most cryptocurrencies. However, what made Litecoin different was the speed at which transactions could be carried out (2.5 minutes), the algorithm on which it was built (scrypt), and some more technical factors which I'll break down as we go along.

Litecoin was created in a manner that ensures the volume of Litecoin in circulation cannot exceed 84,000,000 versus Bitcoin's 21,000,000. This fixed cap shields the currency against hyperinflation and enables its self-regulatory abilities. Everytime a transaction is verified, the network is more secure. To help you understand the technical uniqueness of Litecoin, we go back to the basic foundation of cryptocurrencies we discussed before. Cryptocurrencies are made of code, which make use of algorithms. Litecoin makes use of scrypt hashing algorithm. This algorithm makes it a lot easier for miners to access the system and create blocks faster than with Bitcoin. This has the ability to encourage inexperienced miners to participate in the Litecoin system, and will thus help this alternative coin (or altcoin) be more widely used.

In mining Bitcoin, which are based on the SHA-256 algorithm, a large amount of a computer's processing power is needed. However, for the scrypt-based Litecoin, less powerful computers are needed. The protocol on which Litecoin is constructed makes it easier for consumer-level GPUs to decode it, unlike Bitcoin. This makes Litecoin mining feasible even for the average user. Even some computer manufacturers have begun offering machines with AMD processors which are designed specifically for Litecoin mining. This ease of mining, in combination with the fact that there will be a higher number of Litecoin in circulation than Bitcoin (84,000,000 Litecoins, and 21,000,000 Bitcoins) can cause a lot of miners to transition to mining Litecoin, as the Bitcoin algorithms keep getting harder and harder to crack.

Remember what we said mining was? Miners make use of computers to solve mathematical problems, and these algorithms, when solved, cause more cryptocurrencies to be added to the network and the miners get a reward for their work. Litecoin makes use of proof-of-work to verify transactions which makes mining quite costly in terms of time and energy. As with Bitcoin, all Litecoin transactions are included in a block – the group of transaction entries. Anyone on the Litecoin network has complete access to the information in the blockchain. Again, although the users are anonymous, all transactions are public knowledge. The Litecoin blockchain creates a new block 7.5 times faster than Bitcoin, which is what makes Litecoin transactions faster.

However, this has changed with the activation of Segregated Witness (SegWit) in the Litecoin blockchain. SegWit is a process that enables blocks to be made smaller by extracting signature data from all transactions in the blockchain. The implication is that Litecoin can process incredibly fast payments, so incredibly fast that a few months ago, on 11 May 2017, the Litecoin network was used to send money from Zurich, Switzerland to San Francisco, USA in less than one second! How's that for fast?

November 2013 is probably the most historic month in the history of Litecoin. It grew by over 100% in 24 hours and then reached US$1 billion market capitalisation in the same month. In the same month, Litecoin version 0.8.5.1 was released to enhance the security of the network and to fix some vulnerability issues. In December 2013, the Litecoin developer team released a newer version which offered further reductions in transaction fees, along with more security and performance improvements.

Litecoin vs other coins

Bitcoin, being the first and most popular digital currency, has all of its flaws and weaknesses exposed to the world. Litecoin developers have made it their duty to solve those shortcomings by turning Bitcoin's weaknesses into Litecoin's strengths. I mentioned some of these earlier, like Litecoin's better and faster blockchain due to a more efficient blockchain system than other digital currencies. Merchants would obviously prefer the faster and more secure transactions offered by Litecoin.

Litecoin Wallet

As with other cryptocurrencies, Litecoin's wallet is the digital system that stores your coins and helps conduct and keep track of all your transactions, just like when you send emails. There are different kinds of digital wallets and several exchange systems that deal with Litecoin.

When you buy Litecoins from any of the exchanges mentioned below, you need a wallet to store them. There are several types of wallets, and they appeal to different kinds of users:

- **Web Wallets**: This refers to online wallets that store your Litecoins on someone else's server. You access your coins from anywhere in the world and from any device. You just need to sign in to the server with a password and *voilà*, your coins are right where you left them – unless the company server has been hacked and all the coins stolen (refer to Mt. Gox mentioned earlier). However, these wallets are amongst the most popular type.

- **Desktop/Mobile Wallets**: These are different from the mobile apps of web wallets because they actually store your coins on your device. They are considered pretty safe because to steal them, the thief must have physical access to your device. However, these ones are easy to misplace, and forgetting your phone or laptop in the airport lounge is more likely to give you a heart attack.

- **Hardware Wallets**: These are little pieces of hardware (much like some wire transfer tokens) that can be connected to your computer using a USB cable. These allow you to conduct completely secure transactions because all the really delicate stuff is done offline. These kinds of wallets come highly recommended and highly priced.

A lot of hardware wallets, such as TREZOR or Ledger Nano S, are not free. Some of the non-hardware wallets charge fees for various transactions, and some are completely free. The key is to understand the fine print when choosing a wallet; before clicking that "I agree" tick-box you should understand that those fees can accumulate into a significant amount.

The following list shows some of the Litecoin wallets that have come in highly recommended by users, tech reviews and some relatively random 'experts'.

- **Liteaddress.org** is 'great for those looking for a way to easily store their Litecoins offline.' How it works: the site generates a Litecoin key and address for you which you would use when you want to stash coins. You would need to print the key and address and safely store your Litecoins offline. The concept makes sense, as it is one way to prevent any potential theft.

- **Litecoin-QT** is a desktop wallet that's also very easy to acquire and use. Once you download the desktop application and begin to use it, your computer effectively holds all your litecoins, so make sure you guard the computer jealously. You should probably leave it under your bed at home so no disaster comes near it. Litecoin-QT is one of the wallets that is 100% free to use – no fees, no worries.

- **LoafWallet** is a mobile application currently available on the iOS App Store and has been available for over a year .The Android version is still in development at the time of writing and hopefully, it will be made available soon. The application is one of the easiest wallets to use and even a newbie can find his or her way around the app within minutes.

- **Electrum LTC** is a special wallet that grants a new level of security. It is a web-based wallet which has the ability to generate offline wallets if the user pleases. If a user happens to misplace their wallet, the wallet can always be restored in the desktop and mobile application through a twelve-word seed. The Electrum LTC address key can even be exported to another Litecoin wallet, as it has support for key importation.

Other wallets include Block.io, Exodus and Jaxx, and I will be talking more about some of them in subsequent chapters.

Challenges facing Litecoin

"A lot of people have been saying that SegWit is unsafe because SegWit coins are 'anyone-can-spend' and can be stolen. So lets put this to the test. I put up $1MM of LTC into a SegWit address. You can see it's a SegWit address because I sent and spent 1 LTC first to reveal the redeemscript. Let's see if SegWit really is 'anyone-can-spend' or not. Good luck."

That little note was from a random Litecoin millionaire who put up a $1 million bounty for anyone who could successfully hack into the Litecoin network to steal the money. As at the time of writing this book, the money wasn't stolen – probably meaning it was not successfully hacked. Does that mean Litecoin cannot be hacked? No, it doesn't. The only thing it shows is that people have concerns about the security of Litecoin, as with any other crypto, but the security is much stronger than people think. As with anything based online, hacking and security will always be a concern, and that is one of the challenges facing Litecoin.

Another challenge is the zilchvalue theory. Although very unlikely to happen, it is theoretically possible for Litecoin (and other cryptocurrencies) to become worthless. This can happen if investors decide that they are done with the currency and decide to abandon its use. It can also happen if there is a general decline in the outlook of the world economy that can affect the general cryptocurrency industry. Even though Litecoin has a lot of safeguards put in place to prevent being affected by economic issues, the market is still ruled by human behaviour. There is always a slim chance that everyone can just decide they are no longer dealing with Litecoin, and that would be the end of the currency.

Another challenge that could face Litecoin is change in value. Litecoins are currencies used for purchases and online payments, but they are also a commodity – just like silver or gold. This implies that Litecoin is just as susceptible to market fluctuations as any other commodity or stock – maybe more. The value of the commodity can go up based on increased demand, and can drop as a result of lower demand. Although the supply of Litecoin is highly regulated, the demand side of the currency can cause values to rise and fall.

All litecoins are encrypted to ensure their security. The encryption identifies the coins, but not the owner of the coins. As I said earlier, cryptocurrencies maintain the anonymity of their owners. However, this creates a situation in which if the coin were to be stolen, or mistakenly transferred to the wrong person, it would be impossible to reverse the transaction unless the other party returned the funds voluntarily. Refer to the section on the challenges of Bitcoin to see how this can happen.

Needless to say, the challenges highlighted above are not unique to Litecoin. They are the same challenges faced by pratically every cryptocurrency.

Why might people invest in Litecoin?

The key to investing in Litecoin as with many other traditional investments in the world is to buy low and sell high. The important question is why would someone buy Litecoin versus another cryptocurrency like Bitcoin? Litecoin has been termed as the more "practical" cryptocurrency for every-day use but Bitcoin is the first cryptocurrency to go mainstream and continously attracts widespread media attention. It has been the focal point and is often included in the headlines whenever there are significant developments in the world of cryptocurrencies. Many consider Litecoin to be the "silver" to Bitcoin's "gold". The price of Litecoin as with most other cryptocurrencies is driven by supply and demand, if Litecoin is to be used more often than Bitcoin or other currencies in the future, then Litecoin would be the proper investment choice. The difficult task is determining which cryptocurrency will survive the coming years among the thousands that have recently emerged and the others that have yet to be released.

In the United States, Coinbase is widely acclaimed as the easiest and best option for buying Litecoin. You can link your bank accounts and credit/debit cards and even do wire fund transfers, which is very convenient. There are a few other exchanges that would be useful for a US resident – like Kraken and Gemini. Since Litecoin transactions cannot be reversed once they are transferred, you need to verify your account with proper identification and a few other details.

For trading to/from other local currencies, there's Bter, OKCoin, and BTC China, all from China; BTC-e from Russia and several others. These exchanges also accept trading from other cryptocurrencies, so you can trade from Bitcoin, Ether, Dogecoin, and others into Litecoin.

The Future of Litecoin

The Chinese like it "Lite": one information that needs to be noted when considering the future of Litecoin is the fact that the People's Bank of China has created a new fee structure that stopped all forms of margin trading and introduced a fee on all transactions. This is important to note because China has been a major determinant of price movement for both Litecoin and Bitcoin in the past few years. With these new market rules, Chinese traders would only be able to trade spot positions and the only way for them to make profits is to buy low and sell high. They would need to overhaul their previous strategies and come up with new ones. As it is now, the traders cannot short by selling coins they do not have.

Continuing in relation to the Chinese market is the fact that two major coins dominate the market – Bitcoin and Litecoin. Given the choice between the two markets and the lower prices of Litecoin, traders would have a better chance at having higher percentage gains from small market positions within LTC. In layman's terms, accumulating Litecoin is so much cheaper (and can be more profitable percentage-wise) than accumulating expensive Bitcoin. Litecoin is the only other alternative currency that trades more volume in fiat (traditional) currency than Bitcoin, and the majority of Litecoin's trade volume comes from the Chinese Yuan – which further means that the market for Litecoin can finally become independent of that of Bitcoin.

#LiteHashGrowth: One of the most recent developments in Litecoin is the growth in the network's hash rate. In certain instances, the price of the coin is directly related to the quantity of hashing power on the network. As the network continues to increase in difficulty as a way of regulating the production of coins, miners would be compelled to upgrade their equipment to be more efficient. If the cost of mining coins is greater than the price, then they would hoard coins to create a scarcity, and thus lower the supply of the coins on the market. Soon enough, the prices would rise and the market would be active again.

SegWit and a Roadmap: In March 2017, the scaling solution – SegWit – was activated. It was also in the same month that Coinbase added support for Litecoin which was a big boost for the network. Litecoin's introduction of SegWit before competitors such as Bitcoin might completely change the dynamics of the network and attract a lot of attention from crypto-dealers. Capitalising on this latest development, the Litecoin Foundation released a roadmap that shows new plans to expand the Litecoin project and enable easy adoption and accessibility by new users. From the perspective of the founder, Charlie Lee, the most important near future goals are 'Smarter Contracts.' We will discuss Smart Contracts when discussing Ethereum, but suffice to say for now that Smart Contracts allow coin users to create 'if-then' conditions around how they want transactions to be done, specifically how money should be paid out. Bitcoin users have wanted to have this upgrade for a while, but none of the projects to upgrade the network for this capability have come to fruition. Litecoin, however, already allows for some simple Smart Contract capabilities such as multi-signatures, where two parties are required to be signatories to a payment.

The activation of SegWit allows for the creation of even more complicated scripts such as the smart crypt vault. The smart crypt vault makes use of Merkelized abstract syntax trees and covenants. These scripts create restrictions on how coins are spent, and in combination with creating the smart crypt vault, would allow Litecoin users to create more complex conditions when making payments.

Currently, Litecoin is the fifth-largest cryptocurrency network by market capitalisation. As of the time of writing, one Litecoin is worth about US$61, quite an upward move from the about US$5 price it hovered around just a year ago. Even though Litecoin has the most secure blockchain in the world, it doesn't seem like the market value is reflecting this. Soon enough, it just might.

References

99Bitcoin (2017, July 30). The Complete Guide To Selecting Your Litecoin Wallet. Retrieved from 99Bitcoin.com: https://www.google.com.ng/url?sa=t&rct=j&q=&esrc=s&source=web&cd=1&cad=rja&uact=8&ved=0ahUKEwj586LHhLLVAhWBbBoKHf6FB3cQFggm-MAA&url=https%3A%2F%2F99Bitcoin.com%2Fcomplete-guide-selecting-litecoin-wallet%2F&usg=AFQjCNEA9P7reI6osn7c6tWt8LyUhpNZxQ

Bitcoin.org (n.d.). Bitcoin FAQ. Retrieved from Bitcoin: https://bitcoin.org/en/faq#can-Bitcoin-become-worthless

Buntix, J. (2017, May 2). Top 4 Litecoin Wallet Clients. Retrieved from The Merkle: https://themerkle.com/top-4-litecoin-wallet-clients/

Castor, A. (2017, March 19). SegWit Activation Complete, Litecoin Charts a Course for the Future. Retrieved from CoinDesk: https://www.coindesk.com/segwit-activation-complete-litecoin-charts-a-course-for-the-future/

CoinMarketCap (2017, July 30). Cryptocurrency Market Capitalisations. Retrieved from CoinMarketCap.com: https://coinmarketcap.com/currencies/litecoin/

CoinPursuit (2014). Advantages Over Traditional Money. Retrieved from ConPursuit.com: https://www.coinpursuit.com/pages/advantages-over-traditional-currency/

Hertig, A. (2017, February 7). Inside MAST: The Little Known Plan to Advance Bitcoin Smart Contracts. Retrieved from coindesk: https://www.coindesk.com/inside-mast-little-known-plan-advance-bitcoin-smart-contracts/

Hertig, A. (2017, May 2). The Litening: Will Litecoin be the first Big Blockchain with Lightning? Retrieved from coindesk: https://www.coindesk.com/could-litecoin-be-the-first-major-blockchain-with-lightning/

Litecoin Mining (2015, June 16). What is Litecoin mining? Learn all you need to get started. Retrieved from BitcoinMining.com: https://www.bitcoinmining.com/what-is-litecoin-mining/

Litecoin Trading Exchanges. (2017, June 30). Retrieved from CoinGecko: https://www.coingecko.com/en/coins/litecoin/trading_exchanges

Litecoin.info (n.d.). Time Warp Attack. Retrieved from Litecoin.info: https://litecoin.info/Time_warp_attack

Reiff, N. (2017, July 21). Could Litecoin Be a Better Investment Than Bitcoin. Retrieved from Investopedia: http://www.investopedia.com/news/could-litecoin-be-better-investment-bitcoin/#ixzz4oA0npou0

ricancoin (2017, June). 4 reasons why Litecoin could make a comeback in 2017. Retrieved from Steemit.com: https://steemit.com/litecoin/@ricancoin/4-reasons-why-litecoin-could-make-a-comeback-in-2017

Rocky (2017, January 26). 4 Reasons Why Litecoin Could Make A Comeback In 2017. Retrieved from Cryptohustle: https://cryptohustle.com/4-reasons-why-litecoin-could-make-a-comeback-in-2017

Scott, A. (2014, August 27). 10 Reasons Why Bitcoin is Better than Paypal. Retrieved from CoinTelegraph: https://cointelegraph.com/news/10-reasons-why-bitcoin-is-better-than-paypal

Ševčík, P. (2017, June 28). Paralelní Polis doporučuje Litecoin jako prostředek platby. Retrieved from Paralelni Polis: https://www.paralelnipolis.cz/paralelni-polis-doporucuje-litecoin-jako-prostredek-platby/

Southurst, J. (2017, May 14). Litecoin $1 Million Bounty Invites Hackers to Test SegWit Security. Retrieved from BitsOnline: https://www.bitsonline.com/litecoin-million-challenge-segwit/

Wealth Daily (2017, 07 28). 3 Reasons to Buy Litecoin. Retrieved from WealthDaily: https://www.wealthdaily.com/resources/3-reasons-to-buy-litecoin/93

Chapter 4: Ethereum

To anybody outside the world of cryptocurrencies, that's a rather nerdy-looking guy holding up a page of his math homework. To those on the inside however, it was irrefutable proof that Vitalik Buterin – *the* Vitalik Buterin – was alive and well. Phew!

Who the heck is Vitalik Buterin and why should you care? Let's start from the beginning, shall we?

In 2011, a teenager from Toronto became aware of Bitcoin, and soon got involved by writing blogs for a Bitcoin magazine. This earned him 5BTC per article, (at the time this translated into around US$3.50), so not exactly a fortune. But then, suddenly, in 2013, the price of Bitcoin skyrocketed and the rest, as they say, is history. Soon the teenager, Russian-Canadian Vitalik Buterin, decided to create a new cryptocurrency that would take Bitcoin technology one step further. He wanted a platform that was crypto-economically secure and could facilitate the development of applications that are decentralized. His aim was to build a waste-free and secure network that was better than the Bitcoin network. He went on to conceptualize his idea, Ethereum, by coming up with a white paper which outlined the principles and applications of the Ethereum network which was published in late 2013.

Early in 2014, Buterin announced the launching of Ethereum on a Bitcoin Talk forum page, and this was followed by the launch of a pre-sale for Ether (Ethereum's cryptocurrency token, which can be transferred between accounts, is used to compensate participant nodes for computations performed, and is used to fuel the network). We can compare Ether to an automobile which moves within the Ethereum platform and is usually sought after by investors and developers who want to build and run various applications within the Ethereum platform. There was an overwhelming response to the launch and pre-sale. In April 2014, Buterin unveiled the first 'dummy' of the Ethereum network accompanied by the actual specification of the Ethereum Virtual Machine.

Ethereum was then launched in 30 June 2015 and has become a large and well established decentralized platform which allows development of distributed applications and the convenient execution of Smart Contracts.

How it works

For this blockchain to effectively work, a code which can enable the exchange of items of value like money, property, and shares is required. It uses something called a Smart Contract, which is basically a computer protocol that facilitates, verifies, or enforces the performance of a contract. When the code (Smart Contract) is run on the blockchain, it executes when the set conditions are met and can only operate as it is set without interference from third parties or possibility of downtime. To use a simple example: say two people placed bets on the outcome of the World Series, entrusting a certain amount of digital currency to the system. The system would then check the final score of the game via the web and distribute the funds appropriately. This protocol manages the online exchange, enforces it, ensures performance of both parties is as set, and also handles payment of fees and services.

Miners in Ethereum blockchain work to earn Ether which, apart from simple trading, can also be used to pay for services done by application developers on its network. It is quite different from Bitcoin and other cryptocurrencies when it comes to its capability and purpose. In the case of Ethereum, a program code of any application that is decentralized can be run on it without its ownership being tracked like in the case of Bitcoin, where online payments are enabled by an electronic cash system which uses a peertopeer connection.

The use of a peer-to-peer digital currency limits an individual as they can only conduct specific operations. In order to allow other operations to take place, one has to expand functions of the cryptocurrency or set up a whole new blockchain, which has proven to be really time consuming. The Ethereum network however accommodates any program in whatever programming language, as long as it has enough memory and time to process it. This allows the development of different applications in one blockchain, instead of having to build a new blockchain each time to accommodate a new application.

The programming language applied in Ethereum allows transactions to take place within seconds unlike some other cryptocurrencies where transactions take several minutes.

In July 2016, Ethereum suffered a 'hard fork' or a split as a result of an attack on its most notable project, the Distributed Autonomous Organization (DAO). Earlier that year, the DAO had raised US$150 million through a sale, whereby investors sent money – Ether – to the DAO in exchange for voting tokens. The voting tokens entitled investors to vote on how the DAO would disperse those funds. Just before the votes were held, the DAO was hacked and the hackers were able to move the funds to another account they controlled. The majority of the Ethereum community voted to change Ethereum's code to get the funds back to investors – and away from the hackers. The more vocal minority however, continued to mine the old version of the blockchain. The result was that there were now two slightly different versions of Ethereum available to users – Ethereum, the 'official' version of the blockchain maintained by its original developers, and Ethereum Classic, an 'alternative' blockchain maintained by a wholly new team, where funds transferred during the DAO debacle were never returned to Ether owners.

Both offer the same technology platforms, and according to developers, they are in agreement on a formal roadmap for steps forward. But, the small differences have created two markets, both with a combined value of roughly US$1.4 billion.

Why Ethereum is unique

The emergence of cryptocurrencies has enabled the decentralization of services through various applications. These services include registering titles, voting systems, Etc. In addition to decentralizing services, the Ethereum network can also be used to build decentralized organizations. These are types of organizations which are run by Smart Contracts on a blockchain. Instead of having a structure for the organizational hierarchy and rules to be implemented by people, the code is usually designed to perform these activities, eliminating the need for centralized control and people which is common in traditional organizations. This type of organization that is run on a blockchain network that is not structured on ownership through the usual equity shares, but the buying of tokens that give individuals the right to vote. Also, as long as this organization can sustain its cost of survival and provide services to the people subscribing to it, it can stay on the network.

One of the properties of the Ethereum blockchain is that it is immutable, meaning the data running on its network cannot be tampered with by a third party or any other individual. However, if a mistake is made when writing the code or an attack is made on the network, it can only be corrected by re-writing it, which is against the essence of immutability.

Another aspect is that applications run on the Ethereum platform can never experience down time or be switched off, and due to cryptography they are highly secure against fraudulent operations and hacking, and have no central failure point. These applications are based on consensus, which means decisions are only made by people who have voting rights and who must have some sort of agreement before they can move forward. This makes the platform relatively tamperproof and corruption free.

How to exchange Ethereum

As with other cryptocurrencies, Ethereum is bought and sold via online exchanges. The procedure for buying it is similar to that of Bitcoin, where an exchange platform is decided on, and then the buyers and sellers create an account on it. The account needs to be verified, after which you deposit funds into the account via wire or bank transfers. Once the account has been verified and money is loaded into it, you can go ahead with your buy/sell transaction.

Despite the fact that Ethereum is growing at an impressive rate, most online exchanges do not allow its direct purchase. The easiest way to purchase it is by buying Bitcoin and trading that for Ether through the exchange. However, there are a few exchanges that allow the direct buying of Ether. Examples include:

- **Coinbase**: This platform is widely known for Ether and Bitcoin exchanges. Its users, mostly based in Canada, Europe, and the United States can make an Ether purchase using a connected bank account. Those in Europe are able to buy using their debit or credit cards, with security being ensured through encryption as with normal e-commerce transactions.

- **Bittylicious**: No, not a 'Hello, Kitty' site, but another cryptocurrency exchange which enables users to buy Ether using Euros or British pounds.

- **Kraken**: One of the more popular sites. This exchange is Europe-based and offers a variety of payment methods where Ether can be bought in different currencies including, US dollars, Canadian dollar, Euro, British pound and the Japanese Yen.

- **Coinimal**: This exchange allows buying of Ether using a credit card, Skrill, Sepa or a Neteller debit card in Europe.

- **Bitrush**: This exchange allows buying and selling of Litecoin, Ethereum and Bitcoin in Belgium and the Netherlands.

- **Iconomi**: This exchange allows the use of SEPA (Single Euro Payments Area) transfers to buy Ether in a wider selection of European countries.

It is also possible to buy Ether using PayPal as a payment method. This is a bit of a workaround though, and you would first have to create an account on Virwox – a virtual currency exchange, with its own currency known as Linden Dollars. This is then traded for Bitcoin which is then traded for Ether using any of the discussed methods. Not surprisingly, this method is not widely used or recommended.

Ethereum Wallet

After Ether has been purchased, it can be deposited into a wallet which only the account user has control over. Again, as mentioned when discussing Bitcoin, it is crucial to store Ether in a secure wallet as hacking can occur, leading to the loss of tokens. There are various wallets on which Ether may be stored, including one offered by Coinbase which we discussed earlier. Others include:

- **MyEtherWallet**: This is an open source JavaScript Ether wallet. The website allows users to create, send, and receive Ether without it having any control over their private keys

- **EthereumWallet**: This wallet creates Ethereum addresses on the web browsers of users by using client-side JavaScript. It can be used on Windows, Linux, and Mac.

- **EthAdress**: This is an offline wallet. With it, an open source JavaScript client-side paper wallet is generated. The site creates a private and public key pair which users can then print out and store in a safe place so no external hacker can get the coins.

Why might people invest in Ethereum?

Unlike other stock and bond investments, Ether has no payouts. It is however a great investment vehicle for passive investors, as it has shown considerable growth year after year. It is expected that this growth will remain steady as companies are investing in the currency at an impressive rate. That is not to say it hasn't had its fair share of fluctuations and falls. Far from it. In fact, there was a time when people thought Ethereum was finished as a currency. Which brings me back to the story at the beginning of this chapter.

In June 2017, there was a rumor that Buterin, Ethereum's creator, had died in a car crash. The news caused the price of Ethereum to fall sharply. In order to prove he was indeed alive, Buterin took that selfie with the unique hash for a block created on that day written on a piece of paper. Since it's impossible to find out the hash for a block before it exists, that piece of paper was Buterin's way of saying "Look, I'm alive on the day this hash was created." Aside from the hoax, Ethereum has also had a torrid time in 2017, but bounced back.

Considering that it is an internet currency, it is advisable to be cautious when investing in it. However, I would say that the inherent potential in the use of Smart Contracts makes it quite valuable, in that it is likely to be adopted by many corporations since it decreases processing times for financial and legal transactions, while at the same time increases the processing capacity of the corporation. There have been some impressive Ethereum projects, which point to the potential of this cryptocurrency. The creation of *Enterprise Ethereum Alliance* earlier on in 2017 has led to its price rising significantly. This is because the alliance has given Ethereum popularity within the business network as it enables the tracking of contracts.

A significant project surrounding Ethereum is the partnership between ConsenSys and Microsoft which aims at offering the Ethereum blockchain as a service where prospective clients can have a cloud-based environment to operate on.

Some of the projects being undertaken within the decentralized applications feature of Ethereum include:

- **uPort**: This offers a solution to the problem of losing all data stored on one platform. An individual using it would be able to safely store most, if not all, of their encrypted data on Ethereum's blockchain without fear of losing it. The data stored here can also be shared with anyone at any place and at any time.

- **Augur**: This platform allows users to buy and sell shares of an event's outcome after a successful prediction on the market i.e. if you predict a correct win or loss then you get a reward if your prediction was correct (more on this in the chapter on Augur).

- **Status**: This particular platform will allow users to have access to various applications running on the network and directly interact with them. This acts like WhatsApp messenger as it incorporates the normal messaging structure and one can easily create and maintain a profile or wallet which can be used to access the Ethereum network. The objective of this kind of platform is to reduce the barrier to entry to the Ethereum network while allowing a kind of Ethereum decentralized application on a smartphone.

- **WeTrust**: This platform aims at being a sort of savings and credit service by making utmost use of Smart Contracts. It will enable the creation of a savings and credit association on the public Ethereum network, and will act like a joint savings account for family or friends whose funds can be used in the event of an emergency or in any other event that requires a huge amount of funds. Its main objective is to create more privacy and more control of financial data.

These are just a tip of the iceberg when it comes to the use of Ethereum and Smart Contracts. In fact, it could well be said that Smart Contracts are the next big thing, as they have a variety of uses and are being implemented in various sectors. In insurance for instance, it can be used to significantly reduce the time the claims process takes. Insurance companies can automate insurance policies by writing them into a Smart Contract. They simply specify that when a certain condition of the Smart Contract is met (e.g. a natural disaster), then the claims process is triggered immediately.

Another example is in the real estate industry where real estate agencies are beginning to transfer property transactions onto the Ethereum platform. Thus, all information regarding transactions carried out on a particular property is recorded in the blockchain, effectively preventing fraud. At the same time, it speeds up the transfer process as well as transactions related to the property in question.

Yet another application is in relation to copyrighted content. Currently, it can be challenging to know who owns the copyright to an item, such as music for instance. That also affects the ability to effectively distribute royalty payments to those legally entitled to receive them. By keeping copyright information on a blockchain and using a Smart Contract, it would be easier to keep track of all ownership rights. That way, royalty payments are automatically generated and paid whenever the copyrighted material is used for commercial purposes. This is done in real time, and since the information is on the blockchain, all affected parties can instantly reflect this in their accounting.

The possibilities, it seems, are endless.

Challenges facing Ethereum

But just like any new technology, Ethereum faces some barriers to being adopted widely. Some of these barriers include:

- **Customer usability**: It is difficult to communicate what exactly Ethereum is, especially to individuals who are not familiar or conversant with technical terms. Also, public relations surrounding Ethereum has not been as well developed as is the case with Bitcoin, which means there's less public knowledge about it. Another problem is that there is not much information on Ethereum, as it was only launched recently. It is also difficult for individuals to directly trade in Ether since there are not many major exchanges that list it. Lastly, confidence in the storage security is still a factor that needs to be looked at.

- **Competition**: Another big problem facing the adoption of Ethereum is that it is a challenge when trying to convince competing industries to operate on a similar network which shares market information concerning their products. Companies fear losing their competitive advantages. Another difficult aspect is convincing regulators that codes written and operated on computers can actually manage some aspects of crucial financial markets without the necessity for a third-party regulator.

Since the launch of the Ethereum network, there has not been a single decentralized application developed that would take the technical world by storm, and that could help address some of these concerns. On the other hand, even if an outstanding application is actually developed, the advantages of it being decentralized on this platform still need to be clarified.

The existence of Bitcoin in the market also poses as a challenge to furthering the growth of Ethereum because some of these exchanges make a lot of money from Bitcoin, thus they have no incentive to support further progress of Ether in the cryptocurrency world.

Another obstacle facing Ethereum as with other cryptocurrencies would be the fact that Ether cannot be preferred against stable, known currencies and modes of exchange like gold. People like what they're familiar with. Thus, people would still prefer to stick with the 'status quo' and the familiar when it comes to wealth creation and payments, than risk it all on this new form of currency.

Further barriers to the use of Ethereum are its evident flaws, which can be narrowed down to the following:

- The codes applied here are meant to facilitate different transaction to run on one platform. This makes the network lag a bit, considering that these codes are usually complicated, however, optimism developers can reduce the down time associated with coding exists.

- There is no way formally to prove that the Smart Contracts used on this application are actually accurate, as well as the code used on Ether which is used to fuel the network cannot be proven to be correct.

- As discussed under Bitcoin, there is no legal framework surrounding the use of the Ethereum network, since cryptocurrencies are still new concepts which regulatory authorities are still gaining knowledge about.

There are many other risks surrounding the Ethereum network, like the fact that it has not been in existence for a long time, meaning that the foundation is still short of funds. Considering also that Ethereum has gained ground in the cryptocurrency world due to misunderstandings between the developers of Bitcoin, it is not inconceivable that Ethereum might lose growth once Bitcoin stakeholders solve their issues and politics.

Furthermore, the cryptocurrency world is still growing and drawing a lot of interest from technical corporations. Considering the number of cryptocurrencies that have emerged after Bitcoin, it is obvious that the development of these currencies is continuing to grow. Thus, if a developer comes up with a better platform than Ethereum, it would find itself in a tough operating environment, with a limited number of users.

In addition, we cannot ignore the possibility that it will be used by criminals. There are no known rules or regulations that surround the development of decentralized applications, making it possible for scammers to use this platform to construct various schemes to defraud investors of their Ether. And thus ruin the reputation of the network.

Finally, there is of course the overall issue of security. There has been a reported hack on the Ethereum network where the hacker made away with US$31 million worth of Ether. Similarly, if more wallets are hacked, consumer confidence in Ether would be lost, considering that a fully secure and 'unhackable' storage mechanism has not yet been developed.

Just like any innovation in the technical world, the Ethereum network definitely faces stiff competition as the cryptocurrency market is ready for new and more competent developers who are likely to build impressive projects using cryptocurrencies.

Expected downfall

These new developments can lead to one of the inherent risks faced by all cryptocurrencies, i.e. the possibility of Ethereum collapsing. This may never happen, but is a possible occurrence. Some of the reasons that may lead to this collapse include the fact that as the Ethereum network continues to grow, more tokens in the form of Ether will be created, meaning that more funds will be taken out instead of being set aside so that investors can sell them to fund their projects. Thus, more tokens will be used in contracts if the need arises. If this continues and less Ether is stored, then the value will decrease and lead to most investors selling their Ether while they can still make a profit.

Secondly, there are still loopholes in the Ethereum network, and if incompetent developers continue to run programs on the network, then a rise in Ether prices will be insignificant which will potentially result in its downfall. Since the developers of the Ethereum network have begun realizing the problems associated with it, they are now cautious before coming up with new applications. This is causing their network to be left behind as new developers in the market are coming up with projects that cover problems of scalability, privacy, and security of cryptocurrencies being traded and in storage.

It is not unreasonable to believe that when problems facing the Ethereum network can no longer be hidden, many of the users could abandon it and move to more reliable and secure options. This is because cryptocurrencies are growing and being developed consistently, assuring that there will be better options in the future.

Another worrying factor is that the exchanges that allow trading of Ethereum are not stable, which can cause prices to plummet and as a result, the cryptocurrency can be sold hastily in a panic. A sudden increase in users can cause the exchanges to experience downtime as they are trying to accommodate the influx of users who are all interested in buying or selling currencies. When a platform such as an exchange experiences issues with its system, then users are afraid of further losses and would often decide to sell their currencies at considerably lower prices in order to cut their losses.

Survival expectation of Ethereum

Many believe that Ethereum will never reach the heights of Bitcoin or be strong enough to remove it from the position it is enjoying as the number one cryptocurrency based on current market capitalization. It is arguable, however, that Ethereum has so much more potential than what can be seen currently in the cryptocurrency market. It is quite clear that Ethereum is being taken up at a faster rate since its inception than Bitcoin was. Just two years since its launch, countries have shown interest in the new currency because of its uniqueness. China, for instance, has announced that it intends to come up with a digital yuan which would be based on the Ethereum network. Russia has also shown interest in adopting the cryptocurrency in its various business structures. New Zealand also unveiled its plans to include Ethereum in its digital currency exchanges. The United Kingdom has also not been left behind, as it plans on adopting a new digital asset that will be backed by gold and bets on either Ethereum or Bitcoin.

Such interest from countries and a high rate of interest in Ethereum by investors suggest that this cryptocurrency has a promising future.

References

Arjun, K. (2017, May 26). Ethereum is Headed For A Big Correction After 38% Price Rally, Say Analysts. Retrieved from https://www.cnbc.com/2017/05/26/Ethereum-price-correction-bitcoin.html

Coppola, F. (July 2016) A Painful Lesson For The Ethereum Community. Retreived from https://www.forbes.com/sites/francescoppola/2016/07/21/a-painful-lesson-for-the-Ethereum-community/#351d68f5bb24

Gosh R. et al. Bitcoin or Ethereum? The Million Dollar Question. Retrieved from http://www.economist.com/sites/default/files/carey_business_school_submission.pdf

Medium, 'A beginner's guide to Ethereum.' Retrieved from https//medium.com/blockchannel/Ethereum/

Perry, A. (2017, June 12) Ethereum is dropping, here is why. Retrieved from https//wealthydaily.com/Ethereum/

Stack Exchange. 'Ethereum risks.' Retrieved from https//Ethereum.stackexchange.com/

'The Ethereum project.' Retrieved fromhttps://www.Ethereum.org/

'Ethereum news.' Adopted from https://cointelegraph.com/tags/Ethereum/

Chapter 5: Augur

If you understand how crystal balls work, you'll understand Augur, because that's basically what it is. Kind of. It's just a little more advanced.

Augur refers to a prediction market platform that is fully open-source in addition to being decentralized. It bases forecasts about the outcomes of future events on information that is collected from the crowd (open-source). Before we go further here's something you need to understand: a prediction market is like the stock market, except that you don't buy any stock in a company. Instead you're buying 'stock' in the outcome of events. For example, will the Blue Jays make it to the World Series? Augur is built on Ethereum technology and also works by executing Smart Contracts. The principle that Augur utilizes in forecasting the outcome of events is referred to as the 'wisdom of the crowd' principle, whereby members of the crowd make predictions and these predictions are averaged in order to create the possibility that is most realistic.

The network rewards predictions that are correct while those that are incorrect are penalized as a way of motivating people to report truthfully. Augur is hence distinct as a cryptocurrency based on its reliance on Ethereum and concentration on prediction markets. Augur has an objective of transforming prediction markets and in the process, altering the manner in which people receive as well as value the 'truth.' The technology seeks to create predictions that are more accurate based on information that has been collected from large groups of individuals rather than from a section of experts.

The foundation of its philosophy, if technology can be said to have philosophies, is blockchain technology. Blockchain, as you now know, is like the world's register that archives every transaction in cryptocurrencies, and its operations occur without any central authority controlling them. The open nature of a blockchain creates an opportunity for numerous people to make predictions in a market that does not contain too many regulators. Augur is founded on this idea whereby any individual is allowed to launch or become a part of these prediction markets. The uniqueness of Augur is that it enables all manner of individuals to trade together in a way that was not possible before. Furthermore, wisdom of the crowd facilitates the development of predictions that are more accurate as well as specific since the individuals who participate 'put their money where their mouth is.'

The way Augur works is that once a group of individuals become part of a prediction market and place bets on a specific outcome, Augur pays other individuals to identify the result of the event in order to ascertain the outcome. However, the pay made by Augur is not a flat fee. On Augur's blockchain, it houses a distinct currency – REP. REP is a digital token that's used to motivate individuals to be truthful because if the individual does not tell the truth, they will lose money. This cryptocurrency is not for buying and selling things but instead it follows the user's reputation – an individual who often tells the truth gets higher reputation. Individuals are expected to bet their REP tokens that their prediction is the truth hence indicating that they are reporting facts just as they are. If a large number of people agree, then the Augur system gives back their tokens and cash as payment. The primary objective is to align the objectives of all people in one direction especially since the REP tokens are linked to real money.

So for example, you could have a prediction on whether Dunkirk would win the next Oscar for 'Best Movie.' It would work as follows: a market would be opened in which possible answers to the question (yes or no) are 'stocks' that cost anywhere from 1 cent to $1. Automatically, the market price of the 'yes' and 'no' would reflect the possibility of Dunkirk's chances of winning the Best Movie Oscar. So if a share of 'yes, Dunkirk will win' costs 80 cents, then the likelihood of it happening is understood to be 80 percent. If Dunkirk does go on to win the Best

Movie Oscar, those who guessed correctly then receive a monetary reward for their prediction.

Unlike other cryptocurrencies like Bitcoin, Augur is unique since it aims to leverage more than one blockchain technology in addition to the REP currency that supports its operations, and so it stands as an illustrative model for how future projects can leverage the same designs. As the first open-sourced and decentralized prediction market, Augur anticipates allowing its users worldwide to make bets on the outcome of events that will occur largely in order to encourage collective forecasting. The team that developed this technology seeks to utilize blockchains' decentralized nature to overcome challenges that prediction markets have faced in the past. Centralized management is considered a factor that has significantly contributed to the failure of prediction markets, especially given the influence that global governments have had in shuttering efforts in prediction markets.

Augur is built on the Ethereum blockchain and it utilizes Ethereum as a way of removing the requirement for individuals to trust counterparties as well as reduce costs. In addition, Ethereum enhances the resilience of the platform against centralized points of failure. Custodianship of money becomes automated in a way that's similar to trading or funds settlement by use of Smart Contracts. It is based on the platform's design that facilitates operations with minimal trust. Numerous Ethereum calls have to be made on the Augur technology, which may be a challenge. RPC calls made by a user may sometimes be in the hundreds and so could be the messages that are sent between the Ethereum nodes and the user. (RPC refers to a protocol that one program can use to request a service from a program located in another computer in a network.) While these calls are not charged, they take up bandwidth as well as time.

Augur represents an extension to Bitcoin Core's source code and its features include betting as well as consensus mechanisms that are necessary for a prediction market. Augur shares similarities with Bitcoin in order for the technology to take advantage of the security and scalability that Bitcoin offers. There are three token types (also referred to as units) that Augur uses. In order to track every unit, each input and output value field of a transaction is followed by a unit field. While three token types exist, the user possesses a single cryptographic private key. The addresses of Augur are basically base-58 hashes of the technology's cryptographic public keys and based on this system, the user is able to send tokens. Different token types are distinguishable from others by checking the 'unit's' field. Consequently, the user gets to sign transaction information of a REP payment in the same manner that the user would sign a Bitcoin payment. Bitcoin is the first token whereby sidechains are utilized to give the user permission to transfer Bitcoin and create a transaction on the Bitcoin blockchain. The Bitcoin gets locked up in an address and after that a transaction is created on the platform's blockchain. It is hence evident that Augur utilizes cryptocurrencies (like Bitcoin) to function but fundamentally, Augur is not a cryptocurrency *per se.*

The other token type is tradable reputation tokens (REP) that I mentioned before. REP refers to the reliability of a user in predicting outcomes and represents a funding source for Augur. The third token type is one that may be viewed as seigniorage and it applies in prediction plays that occur in long term contexts. The token acts as a hedge to overcome variations in Bitcoin, which is used to purchase shares for making predictions, although as can be seen above, sometimes the internal currency is used.

The future of Augur

In March 2015, the marketing team at Augur released a video on YouTube called "How a decentralized prediction market works" which was narrated by Shooter Jennings, a country artist who is also a blockchain aficionado. That video became the most viewed video on prediction markets in YouTube history and this led the director of marketing at Augur, Tony Sakich, to invite any individual interested in creating or producing a video with content explaining both the mechanics and the potential of prediction markets in general. This, together with all the other partnerships that Augur has with other players like Bitcoin, goes to show the Augur team's willingness and openness to more partnerships in the future.

In the pre-crowdsale period, marketing was a very big and important aspect of Augur. This is due to the fact that Augur acquired investors through token sale. However, this has greatly reduced in the post-crowdsale and development phase. Time and resources invested in marketing is now allocated to other important aspects in the development and implementation of Augur. As it is trying to encourage collective forecasting, Augur aims is to encourage its global users to increasingly make predictions on the outcomes of future events. Augur is also keen on educating the world about the power as well as the potential of prediction markets, but this has been lined up as future projects rather than deadlines for the Augur team.

Augur manipulates the Ethereum blockchain platform to reduce costs like overhead, and eliminates the need for users to trust counterparties, and also enables the blockchain platform to survive central failure points. This is achieved by the blockchain's automation of the fund's custodianship, trading and fund settlement via Smart Contracts on Ethereum. As you will recall, Smart Contracts are the very foundation of Ethereum and the design of Ethereum allows these functions to happen with little or very minimal trust.

The decentralized nature of blockchains is what the development team at Augur aims to manipulate to avoid matters that have in the past affected or plagued the prediction markets. As previous efforts to eliminate these problems have faced roadblocks by global governments and the centralized management of these prediction markets has been viewed as a point of failure, a new model obviously needed.As the first open-source decentralized prediction market, Augur is rare among Ethereum projects and is fundamentally changing the conventional approach to centralized prediction markets. It also represents a compelling example of what future projects will look like, based on the way it aims or intends to leverage multiple blockchain technologies as well as other cryptocurrrencies like Bitcoin to run its operations.

It is important to keep in mind the implications of Augur as an open source project. The possibility of delays are highly likely, thus any date shared in an Augur update is simply an educated or generalized estimate, not a deadline with promised results. In other words, people are unreliable, and so things may change because Brad is getting married and didn't have time to contribute to the project as he had planned, or the whole world went on vacation at the same time. Stuff happens. By its nature however, it's clear that future development as well as upgrades on Augur's functions are imminent.

There are some features that were not in Augur's initial release, but can be expected in future releases including:

- A more mobile friendly user interface (UI).

- State channel trading.

- Allowing markets that are dominated by other currencies, as opposed to just Ether.

- Manipulating the Liquidity-Sensitive Logarithmic Market Scoring Rule or **LS-LMSR** to achieve more than eight outcome markets. It is important to note that this was supposed to be in the initial release but based on the fact that it does not work very efficiently when using an order book and the complexity it adds, it was removed for the time being.

- SmartContracts.com, Town Crier, as well as RealityKeys to serve as first resolver options built in the UI.

Why might people invest in Augur?

As with traditional investment options like hedge funds, real estate, and stocks, investing in Augur may be seen by some as an interesting opportunity based on the product's open and measurable nature. A person wishing to join the prediction markets based on the Augur platform can purchase REP tokens, which is like a fuel that is Ethereum-based and that enhances operations on the Augur platform. Similar to other coins, it is tradeable on the exchanges. There are 11 million tokens presently available and given that they have a much lower price compared to Ether, purchasing them has the potential to generate profits for the user. Half of all trading fees are paid to users who hold REP tokens based on the percentage of REP tokens that the user has, similar to receiving a dividend on a stocks. One way in which REP can be purchased is by finding an individual who purchased REP during the presale and make the individual's reptrader account your own. It is essential to exercise caution when purchasing the REP from another user as some people may take off with the funds sent, without sending anything in return. Official escrow is hence a recommendable method through which to make a purchase of REP tokens.

The second method through which one can purchase REP is by registering with gatecoin.com which purchased REP from numerous presale users. Following verification on the site (security is a priority under this exchange), one can purchase REP there. The tokens that are purchased at gatecoin.com were exchanged for REP following the launch of Augur.

As of July 2017, Augur REP tokens were still trading at Gatecoin OTC (over the counter) at a price of US$18.8. The investors who purchased REP during Augur's crowdsale also get to price REP tokens and make them available to other people who wish to purchase them in a type of secondary market. This is another approach to investing in Augur as opposed to purchasing REP to engage in prediction markets.

Crypto-asset markets are dominated by speculation since there is no certainty regarding the outcome. However, mathematical clarity regarding actual (real world) processes can be utilized to give an impressive framework for investment analysis.

During Augur's crowdsale, 11 million REP tokens were issued to participants. A user that holds one REP has one vote that allows him or her to trade in the prediction market on Augur, in addition to being entitled to half of the trading fees that will come from that market. In this regard, one can calculate a holder of REP's returns through consideration of a metric termed as 'dollar turnover.' This refers to the amount of dollars that are transacted on Augur, based on the apparatus that creates fees for users as well as investor's returns. As an example, if US$1 billion is Augur's turnover in a year, the assumption made is that 1% will be the average market fee of Augur and as such, the dividend that REP holders will get is $1 billion x 0.01 x .5 = $5 million. A user that holds one REP would therefore get $0.45 as dividend, a sum arrived at by dividing the $5 million by $11 million. Based on this assumption, an individual who gets a REP token now, expects to receive $0.45 when the year ends.

Augur represents a better platform compared to other prediction markets due to its decentralized network. Having been built in the Ethereum blockchain and also being decentralized, the Augur platform has no central servers and in this regard, there is no switching it off. An individual from anywhere across the world has the capability of creating a prediction with ease using Augur's platform by asking a question regarding any issue. The market creator is required to offer the market preliminary funding and this pays off as they get 50% of the collected trading fees in the market's lifetime. Since users set fees in the Augur platform, the fees are very low relative to platforms that have been traditionally used in trading and betting.

Another illustration of the benefits that a decentralized network offers is the aspect of crowdsourced reporting. Centralized markets have high probability of mistakes occuring(regarding market outcomes) or being outright manipulated since one individual points out the final outcomes in the market. Augur allows thousands of people to report on market outcomes based on a unique system that is consensus-based and a distinct token – REP. A user who acts as a reporter is allowed to provide reports on events every two months and they are rewarded with 50% of the fees that are in the system multiplied by the percentage of REP that they win.

The payments under Augur are safe and automated as they get stored in Smart Contracts whereby counter-party risk is eliminated. Further, Smart Contracts enable payments to be made quickly and based on automated systems to the traders who have won. Payment automation extends to deposits and withdrawal of funds by use of blockchain. The potential for human error has been eliminated given that human intervention is nonexistent.

Challenges facing Augur

Strong security measures such as Smart Contracts have been put in place to make Augur a highly secure platform. However, hacking is always a major concern given that operations are conducted using digital technology and a hacker may find a way to access a user's personal information. The Augur platform itself is secured against hacking but individual users may become victims of a hack. If the user who gets hacked holds a significant percentage of REP, the Augur platform may be impacted since such a user has the potential to influence the cryptocurrency's value if they move funds. A good example is the recent incident of hacking by an unknown person who managed to steal approximately US$300,000 in cryptocurrency (REP as well as Ether). The hacker gained access to the phone of a user named Bo Shen who holds significant Augur and Ethereum cryptocurrencies. They managed to take over Shen's email address and gained access to the cryptocurrency accounts. When the hacker moved funds that Shen held, trading prices for Augur and Ether were significantly affected. Hacking is hence a possible setback and while it is more of a threat to individual users, the value of cryptocurrency that the hacked user holds may impact the Augur platform negatively.

There is little risk that Augur will collapse, based on safeguards that the technology has and its decentralized nature, which reduces potential intervention by global governments as has been the case in some centralized prediction markets in the past. That's not to say, however, that it can never happen. Of course there's a possibility of collapse as with any other cryptocurrency, and concerns exist regarding the potential collapse of the platform, but so far these are just suppositions that have not been established with facts. Given the large investment that the platform has made on technical skills and the tests that have been perfomed to assure its sustainability, potential investors can have some degree of confidence in the system.

References

Augur (2017). Get rewarded for your knowledge and insight. Retrieved from https://Augur.net/

Brukhman J. (2016). A sane model for pricing Augur REP tokens. Coin Fund. Retrieved from https://blog.coinfund.io/a-sane-model-for-pricing-Augur-rep-tokens-32dbd9db5f6

Cade Metz, Forget Bitcoin. The Blockchain Could Reveal What's True Today And Tomorrow. Retrieved from https://www.wired.com/2017/03/forget-bitcoin-blockchain-reveal-whats-true-today-tomorrow/

Cimpanu C. (2016). Hacker Steals $300,000 from Major Cryptocurrency Investor. Bleeping Computer. Retrieved from https://www.bleepingcomputer.com/news/security/hacker-steals-300-000-from-major-cryptocurrency-investor/

Cruz, K. (2015, April 27). Augur Answers Tough Questions with its Blockchain-based Prediction Markets retrieved from https://bitcoinmagazine.com/articles/augur-answers-tough-questions-blockchain-based-prediction-markets-1430163902/

Krug J. and Peterson J. (2016). Augur: a Decentralized, Open-Source Platform for Prediction Markets. Brave New Coin. Retrieved from https://bravenewcoin.com/assets/Whitepapers/Augur-A-Decentralized-Open-Source-Platform-for-Prediction-Markets.pdf

Chapter 6: Ripple

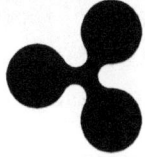

How would you like to see your investment jump a whopping 3,800% within six months? Pipe dream, right? Tell that to the guys who've just seen that happen with Ripple, the best-named cryptocurrency as far as I'm concerned. Simple, un-nerdy and rather playful, I love the name Ripple. As it turns out, there are better reasons to love the cryptocurrency itself. But first, let's back up and give it the proper, whole-history-on-tap treatment, shall we?

Ripple is a digital currency, a technology that operates as both a cryptocurrency and as a digital payment network for financial transactions. Ripple can be described in simple terms as a real-time payment system. It is a distributed, open source payment platform or system whose main goal is to enable people to free themselves of the walled gardens of financial networks, like credit cards and traditional financial institutions for example. These institutions restrict access with fees and processing delays.

How it works

Ripple, released in 2012 and co-founded by Jed McCaleb and Chris Larsen, is known more for its digital payment protocol than for its role as a cryptocurrency. It operates on an opensource and a peer-to-peer decentralized platform that allows for smooth transfer of money in any form. However, despite the existence of such digital currencies as Bitcoin and Ethereum, Ripple still stands out as a result of some of its own unique features. Such features include the fact that it has decentralized exchange facilitation capabilities.

The decentralized platform operates in such a way that there are several payment providers on the system. For instance, Mike is a *Justcoin* customer and his *Justcoin* balance is stored on the Ripple network alongside Nancy and Bruce who have *Bitsmap* balances. Mike wants to buy from Nancy but Nancy is not interested in Mike's *Justcoin* and therefore does not want to sign up with *Justcoin* simply to withdraw her money. Bruce does a lot of business with other *Justcoin* customers and therefore wouldn't mind a *Justcoin* balance. Since Bruce provides authorization for the system to automatically transfer some of Bruce's *Bitsmap* balance to Nancy's account in exchange for Mike's *Justcoin*. Since he's serving as an exchange system for the two different payment providers, he can charge a small fee for this service. This kind of decentralized payment platform used to exist on the Ethereum token, and it now exists on the Ripple network.

The main difference between Bitcoin and Ripple is that Bitcoin was the first successfully implemented peer-to-peer cryptocurrency, whereas Ripple was originally a payment system, a currency exchange, and a remittance network. Over time, it built up its network to include its own currency called Ripples.

As you may recall from the first chapter, Ripple is actually older than Bitcoin, since the project was first implemented by Ryan Fugger in 2004, whereas Bitcoin was first launched by Satoshi Nakamoto in January 2009. However, it was just a payment network and a distributed exchange. It was not until February 2013 that the currency was launched by OpenCoin, Inc., a company created by Jed McCaleb and Chris Larson in order to advance the concept of Ripple. OpenCoin later became Ripple Labs Inc.

The currency on its own has become a success and consequently in the first year of its launch, Ripple had a market capitalization of 2,510,981 BTC.

Furthermore, Bitcoin is created through mining by the users, while Ripple's creators created 100 billion Ripples right from the beginning. Out of the 100 billion Ripples, 20 billion was retained by the creators while the other 80 billion was gifted to Ripples Labs, which retained 25 billion and distributed 55 billion of the 80 billion to charitable organizations, users, and strategic partners. As a consequence of its mining creation process, Bitcoin takes more time to authorize than Ripple, whose transactions are almost instantaneous. However, Ripple transactions are considered as IOUs, which is not different to the conventional banking systems. This basically means that payments are done through transfer of debts (IOU).

In order to buy or sell Bitcoin, one has to use centralized exchanges which could shutdown (remember Mt. Gox, I mentioned earlier?) whilst Ripple is a distributed exchange where one has to buy or sell Ripple on its own secure network. In the event that a direct exchange between two currencies doesn't exist at any given time, Ripple's own cryptocurrency, called XRP, is used as a bridge currency. Its mechanics are actually quite similar to Bitcoin's blockchain technology. This cryptocurrency, XRP, is growing exponentially and at present has the third largest market cap among cryptocurrencies, with Bitcoin and Ethereum having the largest and second largest respectively. Ripple also tracks information of any kind, and it can track account balances of an existing currency while Bitcoin only tracks the movement of Bitcoin. Ripple's transactions are 'free-ish.' That is to say that Ripple charges a fee for its transactions but the fee charged does not go to anybody's pockets because they are destroyed at the end of the transaction. What does that mean?

Well, Ripple transactions have a cost, as with any solution. The cost is meant to combat fake accounts by making it too expensive for spammers to flood the platform with transactions which would render the ledger or blockchain unmanageable and slow the clearing process. To protect the XRP ledger from being disrupted by spam and denial-of-service attacks, each transaction must destroy a small amount of XRP. This transaction cost is designed to increase along with the load on the network, making it very expensive to deliberately or inadvertently overload the network. Every transaction must specify how much XRP to destroy to pay the transaction cost. In other words, while there is a transaction fee, Ripple doesn't really collect the fees the way PayPal, banks, and credit cards do. Rather a small portion of a ripple (equivalent to ~1/1000th of a cent) is destroyed with each transaction rather than retained. The deduction both safeguards the system and reduces supply, causing its valuation to rise.

The team at Ripple has engineered a system of payment like normal cryptocurrency blockchains which processes its transactions using a shared ledger. This network is very efficient as it reduces the time and the cost of clearing by allowing assets to move directly, freely, and instantly. Using the distributed ledger technology, Ripple believes that the cost of transacting for commercial payments and retail remittance will reduce by up to 60%. Another big plus for Ripple is that it works with any size of payment and can be used for cross-border transactions.

The future of Ripple

The invention and application of cryptocurrencies marked a very pivotal point in the history of global payment systems. It laid down a foundation for an Internet Protocol (IP) based payment system. The existing global payment systems were built on the outdated rails of the pre-internet era. Now Ripple wires money globally using the federated payment network and IP which means that anyone can send money anywhere in the world cheaply, instantly, and in almost any currency. While international bank transfers often take about two days to process, it is only a matter of seconds to complete a transaction or a fund transfer with Ripple, which capitalizes on the famous 'small world' philosophy.

Ripple's price has been trending upward and should continue to do so once it gets recognition from more traditional banks as a means of funds and asset transfer as well as foreign exchange. Just a few years ago, no one would have figured that Bitcoin would practically become mainstream, widely accepted and used. Once Ripple gains popularity, its prices will skyrocket as has already been the trend with Ripple and other cryptocurrencies. This could take up to five years or more and in the meantime, the price of Ripple will continue to fluctuate and remain volatile.

Over 60 institutions around the world have embraced Ripple as a means of funds and asset transfer. These include: UBS, UniCredit, Royal Bank of Canada (RBC), Santander, and many more. Cross-border transactions are the biggest selling point for Ripple. The National Bank of Abu Dhabi is the most recent bank to embrace it specifically for cross-border transactions like funds and asset transfers. More and more companies are realizing that Ripple can help them gain efficiency in fund settlement.

The team at Ripple continues to direct time and resources towards improving the network, and growing its global presence by increasing partnerships with global institutions.

A group of banks from Japan embraced the technology and are planning to employ it on a commercial scale by the end of 2017. This means that approximately 40% of commercial banks in Japan will in some way be linked to the Ripple protocol. Further, in 2018, Bank of America Merrill Lynch (BAML), Royal Bank of Scotland (RBS) and other global firms are planning to embrace Ripple for cross-border payments for their commercial and retail customers. So, it's looking like even people who haven't the slightest inkling what blockchain is will soon find themselves transacting using platforms built on the technology. Aren't you glad you're reading this book and getting a head start?

With only five years of experience as a player in the business, it is hard to ignore Ripple's magnificent rise among cryptocurrencies. Working with the assumption that Ripple sticks to the path of other successful currencies like Bitcoin and Ethereum, its price will likely continue to soar.

Investing in the currency

Digital currencies are still in their early growth stage and just like the stock market (and as has been said of the other cryptos discussed), the technique for investing is quite simple: buy low, sell high. This means that many of the people who get rich or draw a lot of profits are those who buy stocks with great potential from companies with a strong foundation and continue to hold these shares through periods of torrid volatility.

There are two ways to make a purchase of XRP: institutional purchases for banks and other payment providers, and individual purchases where individuals can buy the currency using other cryptocurrencies or using fiat currency like the dollar. This can be done through exchanges like Kraken, CoinBase, BitStamp, Gatehub, etc. After purchasing you can store the Ripple XRP on an online wallet like Gatehub.

Critics have argued that the banks, and other payment institutions Ripple has forged partnerships with, are only interested in using the Ripple software and do not have any intention of ever using the XRP. This would therefore mean that the XRP may never really gain much value. Over the long-term, Ripple looks like a high-probability trade based on its trend and the fact that a tiny bit of Ripple is destroyed in every transaction – making the value of a Ripple rise as the number of transactions increase.

Why might people invest in Ripple?

Ripple's value as a cryptocurrency has been increasing greatly over the last few years. When contrasted with different asset classes such as stocks, real estate, and private equity, Ripple is an additional option to consider. One of the reasons that makes Ripple a worthwhile investment over other potential investments is the lower cost of investing. All one has to do is invest and wait for the right time to carry out an exchange. This is different from what happens with other types of investments. With real estate for instance, there are many additional costs that may come with the maintenance of the property. Investing in hedge funds also comes with great costs and very large minimum investment deposits especially when it comes to associated fees. Bill Robertson, a manager on Covestor, an online investment management platform that allows people to mirror the real trades of successful individual or professional investors, also warned about the rising cost of investing in hedge funds. He said that due to the great demand in institutional investing in the industry, there has been a doubling of hedge fund fees as of late.

Unlike other investments, Ripple investing does not require numerous legal procedures since governments do not control it. Other investments such as real estate investments are usually regulated and require the intervention of a lawyer. The absence of legal hoops to jump through makes Ripple easier to invest in.

Passive versus active investing

Sophisticated investors usually carry out a great deal of research before deciding on whether to buy a stock of a company. They have to consider many variables and select the ones that best suit their needs. The same considerations apply when one is looking to invest in Ripple. Investors have to consider the risks that are present with active and passive investment. Unlike investments where the collapse and rise of an asset may take years, the collapse of Ripple could take a matter of weeks or even days, given the nature of cryptocurrencies.

Although the currency has been increasing in value, it's probably better to adopt an active investment strategy on this particular currency given the large supply being held by multiple parties. In seven weeks of 2017, the currency experienced a 57% fall in value from $0.42 on 17 May to a value of $0.18 on 5 July. Prior to the collapse, the currency had risen by 70%, which made it the third largest cryptocurrency. Note that Ripple owns 60% of the XRP and therefore they has the ability to manipulate the currency to their liking. At the moment, the currency is performing well, but what if they decide to flood the market with cheap XRP?

In a report from the founders of Ripple, users were discouraged from speculative investment in the currency. Their exact words were: "Private exchanges and liquidity providers may choose to hold additional XRP for trading. Ripple (the company) **does not** promote XRP as a speculative investment." That could of course just be a disclaimer to cover their backsides from a legal perspective, but they could also have said it based on something they know that you don't. It may therefore be a great risk to invest in the currency over the long term compared to the short term.

Challenges facing Ripple

One of the main barriers of Ripple as a currency is that it is not an open blockchain, which restricts individuals from getting full access to the Ripple network. Most of the other cryptocurrencies we've discussed, like Ethereum and Bitcoin among others, use open blockchains. With Ripple, however, the blockchain is usually closed. You first have to establish trust lines with the other parties and they have to accept you as a trustworthy person before they allow transactions. This process therefore means that you can only carry out a transaction with a limited number of people, only the people you consider trustworthy and vice versa. Considering most of the people who use the currency are banks, they usually have no reason to accept individuals.

Ripples are designed in such a way that they absorb real world assets and send them to the Ripple network. This process of sending the assets to the network is called issuance. After transferring the assets to the Ripple blockchain, banks will transact these issuances with third parties while utilizing the low transaction costs present on the blockchain. These issuances hold real value and in the event a fraudster creates a fake issuance, people on the network will treat it as real. The existence of a fake issuance could lead to a collapse of the network and loss of trust in the system.

The existence of issuance with the use of the currency makes it mainly suitable for Business-to-Business (B2B) transactions. This may hinder the currency from becoming popular since normal, everyday people cannot transact with it freely and may therefore opt for more suitable alternatives.

Another challenge that faces Ripple is that there are doubts about the currency's ability to fulfill the needs of global financial institutions while in its current state. With the permission of Bitcoin developer, Peter Todd, a secretive distributed ledger-consulting group R3CEV, made a report that raised questions on the transaction viability of the currency.

Although the report included some praises for Ripple Lab, there were areas that R3CEV raised concerns pertaining to the open-source technology the company offers. The report indicated that in a scenario where more than 20% of Ripple's network nodes fail to agree, there would be an effective division of the system's ledger. According to the report, what was more troubling was that considering the technology is decentralized in nature, there is a great probability that Ripple will not cause a substantive change to the existing centralized settlement framework. The report states that the centralized model Ripple network possesses fails to eliminate the necessity of a trusted third-party; instead it creates a new kind of third-party. Furthermore, R3CEV stated that using cryptographic tokens through consensus algorithm is effective in creating an 'incentive misalignment' between institutions and Ripple Labs, which places it at odds with the nodes that are active on the Ripple Network.

The other problem briefly mentioned earlier and again in their report is that Ripple is still the highest holder of XRP with a 60% share. The company considers this as a technique to avoid spam that may deter transactions. However, at a time when there are numerous transactions taking place at the same time, the server load is increased, which lowers transaction speed. Slower transaction speeds usually affect the users since it increases the cost of transaction and the amount of XRP required. This problem of Ripple owning 60% of XRP may discourage investing in the currency since they control the market, and can decide when to adjust the cryptocurrency's value.

Other observers have also pointed out that Ripple has vulnerabilities due to its open nature. Some scholars from Purdue University conducted a study on the vulnerability of the currency and established that since the core of the Ripple network remained liquid, it is open to attacks. The liquidity in the network leaves some nodes within the network open to attacks, which may paralyze some of the users' access to funds. According to the study, approximately 50,000 wallets could be paralyzed immediately if an attack were to occur. As with the other cryptocurrencies discussed, there is a chance the Ripple currency may collapse due to its limited blockchain. People are reluctant to use the system since it does not accommodate everyone. This however, is only a supposition and should not be relied upon in making decisions. As with all things, it is best to get as many facts as possible before making a definitive decision. The cryptocurrency has been performing well in the markets and has risen to third place behind the leading cryptocurrencies, Bitcoin and Ethereum.

References

Investopedia (2017, June 14). *Ripple Is Up 3800%: Should You Be Buying?* Retrieved from investopedia.com: http://www.investopedia.com/news/ripple-38000-should-you-be-buying/

Richter, W. (2017, June 12). *Beware of collapsing cryptocurrencies.* Retrieved from businessinsider.com: http://www.businessinsider.com/bitcoin-price-Ethereum-collapsing-cryptocurrencies-2017-7?IR=T

Schuster, B. (2017, May 8). *Ripple – Why You Shouldn't Invest (and Not Because It's a Scam).* Retrieved from hivergent.com: http://hivergent.com/you-shouldnt-invest-in-ripple-and-not-because-its-a-scam/

Pilkington, N. (2017, June 25). *The next big thing?* Retrieved from themarketmogul.com: http://themarketmogul.com/ripple-investments/

Reiff, N. (2017, June 26). *What is the biggest threat to cryptocurrency.* Retrieved from investopedia.com: http://www.investopedia.com/news/what-biggest-security-threat-ripple-cryptocurrency/

Wolff, E. (2017, July 30). *How to buy Ripple (XRP) in 3 Simple Steps – A Beginner's Guide.* Retrieved from 99Bitcoin.com: https://99Bitcoin.com/how-to-buy-ripple-xrp-in-3-simple-steps-a-beginners-guide/

Chapter 7: Dash

Unless you're Darth Vader or you make chocolate, you probably shouldn't name your product *Dark* anything. Our next cryptocurrency – Dash – learned that the hard way.

This cryptocurrency was introduced to the market on 18 January 2014 as XCoin. Its name was then changed and it started being referred to as DarkCoin in February of that year. This was probably meant to reflect the fact that the main objective of this cryptocurrency was to restore privacy in transactions, an aspect many felt other cryptocurrencies had lost. But soon, it became associated with the dark web and so DarkCoin had to change its name again to enable it to distance itself from the criminal tendencies of the dark web. So on 25 March 2015 it became formally known as Digital Cash, *aka* Dash.

Difference from other currencies

This particular cryptocurrency uses a chained hashing algorithm which is known as X11, this makes it different from its counterparts like Bitcoin and Litecoin which use SHA-256 algorithm. Simply, the advantage of using this algorithm is the fact that it allows mining using both GPUs and CPUs.

The X11 algorithm possesses a feature known as the InstantX service. This feature enables an individual to lock his or her inputs to particular transactions and verify these transactions through consensus. The transaction can only fail if consensus is not reached. When the transaction fails, it goes back to the standard process. The InstantX feature enables Dash to solve the long waits that arise when trying to double spend, and this makes it stand out from the number one cryptocurrency at the moment, Bitcoin.

Since the main aim is to restore privacy, Dash uses DarkSend as a method of achieving privacy in transactions. Darksend uses Masternodes which are similar to the tumblers used on Bitcoin. What's a tumbler? Here's a useful explanation courtesy of Wikipedia:

> *A cryptocurrency tumbler or cryptocurrency mixing service is a service offered to*

> *mix potentially identifiable or 'tainted' cryptocurrency funds with others, with the intention of confusing the trail back to the fund's original source.*

For Dash, the Masternode provides this service, so all transactions performed are usually sent to the Masternodes. For similar inputs, they are all put into one transaction accompanied by various outgoing transactions. This process can be repeated a couple of times to increase the obscurity of the transactions.

How it works

The foundation of Dash, just like any other cryptocurrencies, is the blockchain. This acts as a decentralized ledger of all the transactions which have taken place over a certain period of time. The security of this blockchain is improved by a consensus mechanism known as 'Proof of Work' (POW). Once miners are successful and actually solve the mathematical problem posed and the network verifies that the problem is correctly solved, a new block is added to the existing blockchain and the individual miner earns the Dash currency.

There are three unique products associated with the Dash cryptocurrency. These products include:

- **InstantSend:** This is a service that facilitates instant or immediate transactions. It operates by locking inputs belonging to a specific transaction and then verifying these inputs by consensus in the Masternode network.

The various transactions and blocks that are conflicting are rejected. When the consensus needed for verification cannot be reached, the transaction can alternatively be validated through a standard block confirmation i.e the standard process. This product, as mentioned before, saves the time spent on confirmation of double-spending transactions.

- **PrivateSend:** This is the new name for DarkSend, mentioned above. This is a form of coin-mixing service that is based on CoinJoin but with several modifications. Some of the modifications include the use of Masternodes instead of a single website for consensus, and chaining. This is done by mixing with several Masternodes, resisting the pre-mixing and mixing of coins and making it possible to only accept certain denominations like 0.1 DASH, 10 DASH. It also allows passive mode transactions and the maximum allowed for a single PrivateSend transaction is 1000 DASH.

Its features continuously improve with consistent repetition of its processes, and this applies a more advanced method of pre-mixing denominations which are built into an individual user's wallet. The PrivateSend implementation has also allowed Masternodes to submit transactions using a special network code known as DSTX which allows for additional privacy to users.

In its most recent implementation, PrivateSend combines identical inputs from different users into a single transaction, allowing it to restore privacy to transactions. Since the input of the transactions are identical, the transactions cannot be directly traced, making the flow of funds unclear. It also ensures that coins remain of the same value as it allows coins of the same denomination to mix with other wallets.

- **Masternodes:** Dash utilizes a two-tier network, unlike Bitcoin which utilizes a single-tier network, where all the transactions are performed on the network by miners. The application of two-tier network by Dash, makes particular functions, such as the creation of a new blockchain to be done by miners in the first-tier. The second-tier of the network is comprised of Masternodes that perform InstantSend, PrivateSend, and governance functions.

These Masternodes usually need 1000 DASH in order to prevent any Sybil attacks. This is an attack where identities in a peer-to-peer network are forged and used to get majority influence over the network. The 1000 DASH can be spent at any time; once they're spent however, the Masternodes will be removed from that particular network.

Since Masternodes facilitate important network functions, the block reward is usually divided between the miner and the Masternode, each getting 45% of the block reward. The 10% that remains is used to fund the 'treasury' system.

What makes it unique?

Dash stands out as it is the first decentralized autonomous organization powered by a Sybilproof system. Decentralized Governance by Blockchain (DGBB), commonly known as 'treasury or budgetary system,' is a way of reaching a consensus on a proposed network change and funding development of the Dash ecosystem. As mentioned before, the treasury system gets 10% of the rewards so that it can fund projects that will be beneficial to the future of Dash. Funds from this system are used to add to the taskforce and increase the number of developers. It also funds attendance at conferences and integrations with large exchange platforms and API developers.

Every Masternode operator can only vote once when voting for project proposals. The proposals are eligible for funding after following a particular process. In the event that the number of project proposals which comply with the process are more than the available funds, then the proposals with the highest number of votes will be paid for.

Users can interact with the proposal submitters through the official Dash website forums (dash.org). These forums allow the proposal submitters to provide multiple drafts, which are then pitched and vetted for community support before they are finally submitted on the network for a vote. Upon getting enough support, the network is set to automatically release the required funds during the following super block, which is usually after a month.

The funding system has witnessed a huge growth in revenue since its inception in 2015, when it was able to only provide US$14,000 per month in funding. Currently, it has expanded considerably and is now able to pay out US$650,000 per month for different projects. This has created a positive impact where additional developments done through projects increase the value of the currency, thus increasing the amount of funding provided by the revenue system in place.

Exchanges that allow Dash trading

Considering that Dash is a relatively new cryptocurrency that is not widely used like Bitcoin or Ethereum, there are very few exchanges that allow its trading. Some of the platforms that exist include:

- **Kraken:** This exchange was founded in 2011, and is one of the largest exchanges dealing with various digital currencies like Monero, Ethereum, Bitcoin, Litecoin, REP tokens, etc. It allows trades in US Dollars, Euros, Canadian Dollars, Japanese Yen, and British pounds. The upside of using this exchange is that it is secure, with low transaction fees, good exchange rates, and good user support. However, the problems associated with its use include limited payment methods. Also it is not accommodative to new users due to its technicality.

- **Shapeshift:** This is another leading exchange and it supports various cryptocurrencies like Zcash, Monero, Ethereum, Bitcoin, Dogecoin, etc. It offers a conducive environment for users who do not wish to sign up or create accounts or use platforms that hold their cash. It allows instant and direct trades. However, it lacks flexibility such that it does not permit users to buy cryptocurrencies with fiat money, only through the exchange of dash for other cryptocurrencies. Unlike Kraken, it is beginner-friendly, fast, and reasonably priced with a good number of cryptos to choose from.

Dash Wallets

Just like other cryptocurrencies, Dash is stored in wallets that allow Dash owners to receive, store, and send Dash. They are usually simple to use and payments can be sent from the wallets using the Dash feature called PrivateSend discussed above. The options available include:

- **Dash official wallet:** This is the professional dash wallet which contains the full blockchain and is usually seen as a complete node on the network. When it starts up, it requires some time to sync with the blockchain before it can be used. It allows for coin pre-mixing, privacy protection, instant transactions, Masternode integration, Auto back up, and voting or budget proposals. It is available on PC, Mac, and Linux.

- **Third party wallets:** These are wallets that are usually stored by a third-party on a remote server. This allows for easy access of information from anywhere, regardless of the computing device being used. Third party wallets are generally safe, but that's not to say they can't be hacked. So again, buyer beware.

Some of the third-party wallets that can be used to store Dash cryptocurrency are:

- **Exodus**: A multi-currency wallet with an easytouse interface, it allows storage of several digital currencies and gives room for easy organization and calculation of users' savings, using a pie chart. It also has a built-in exchange which allows users to instantly trade the supported currencies. Exodus also has a backup wizard which allows the user to keep the wallet safe and ready for use later on. This platform is partially open source.

- **Jaxx**: Developed by Kryptokit, it allows for trade between Ether, Dash, Litecoin and Bitcoin among other digital currencies. On this platform, the user's funds are not held by the wallet, it offers client-side security model which has private keys that are hosted locally and never sent to any servers. The design of this wallet allows for simple and attractive user experiences. Jaxx uses standards which ensure that in the event the wallet collapses or ceases to exist, the keys can be imported into another service. It safeguards privacy as users are not required to input any personal information like their email addresses. The main focus of the wallet developers is to give the wallet a single screen operation which allows all the wallet functions to work on a single screen. The user does not have to keep on switching between different screens to get the needed wallet address or trying to find the appropriate QR code. It also allows pairing across devices i.e. Mobile, Desktop and Extension through scanning a pairing token.

There are also hardware wallets available which are offline security wallets not kept on any computer, website or server. The hardware wallets usually work with the wallet software on the computer of the user by managing the generation of the private keys, storage of the keys generated and signing of any transactions that occur. Some of the available hardware wallets that support storage of Dash include:

- **Keepkey**: Available on Amazon, it is used to secure different cryptocurrencies such as Bitcoin, Dash, Ethereum, Litecoin, Dogecoin and Namecoin. It ensures that these assets are safe and cannot be tampered with by thieves or hackers. The wallet generates a private key through its random number generator, combined with additional randomness provided by individual computers. After generating the private key, the user is allowed to write down the back-up of the KeepKey, which is usually in the form of a twelve-word recovery sentence. This is only done once. The private key is then stored in the wallet which is PINprotected. This makes it useless if it falls into the wrong hands. When it comes to transactions, each transaction for currencies leaving the device must be approved manually using the confirmation button. It also allows for exchange of digital currencies directly on the device using the Shapeshift platform. If the KeepKey is lost or stolen, it can be recovered without compromising the private keys in any way. It is also malware proof and virus proof. It can work on Android, Linux, PC and Mac.

- **Ledger Nano S**: This wallet ensures security of private keys and sensitive operations are never exposed as it is always locked by a PIN code. The transactions being undertaken cannot be tampered with as they are verified on the screen by pressing a physical button. Using this wallet, an individual who owns Dash can receive and send payments, check their accounts, and manage different addresses for each currency from the same device. Another upside of using this wallet is that it supports the FIDO Universal Second Factor standard, which eases the authentication process on various compatible online services like Dashlane, Gmail, GitHub, or even Dropbox.

- **Trezor**: This wallet bills itself as the original and most secure hardware wallet. With Trezor, extra software is not needed as it supports Dash currency just like Bitcoin. This means that Dash can be added from the drop down menu on the upper left hand corner of the wallet, and it can accommodate other cryptocurrencies such as Zcash, Ether and Bitcoin. The currencies can be easily differentiated as each of them has a unique address.

Why might people invest in Dash?

Dash may be what investors may have been looking for in various cryptocurrencies and associated projects to dive into cryptocurrency investing. Why do I say that? One of the main reasons people consider investing in Dash is that it provides a greater degree of anonymity to the user throughout the entire transaction in comparison with other cryptocurrencies. This presents Dash as a major game changer in the world of cryptocurrencies. Judging by the number of investors in traditional currency who go to great lengths to hide their identities behind shell companies, this may be an alluring alternative.

Another strength associated with Dash is its Masternode two tiernetwork which allows it to include innovations which other cryptocurrencies cannot adopt or develop currently. Such innovations include; InstantSend, PrivateSend and its Treasury system.

The fact that the developer has gone public with the product creates a sense of trust aimed at sophisticated investors. This will surely have an impact on how the cryptocurrency markets operate. Greater support can be obtained for legitimate projects as mutual trust continues to be fostered.

The developer and creator of the currency has a commendable track record when it comes to successfully realizing improvements to the crypto space surrounding Dash. Furthermore, the Dash team provides coherent and regular information concerning the technical aspects of the product. The information provided is usually relayed in layman's terms for those who are less technically-inclined.

Another positive development is the recent announcement of a partnership with Wall of Coins which allows users to buy and sell Dash at banks such as Bank of America, Chase, and Wells Fargo, including financial service companies like Western Union and MoneyGram. On the Wall of Coins platform, users can buy Dash with cash or sell Dash for cash. The customers are instructed to deposit cash at a local financial institution from the website and after a short period of time will directly receive Dash in their preferred software wallet.

The individuals using Dash, referred to as the Dash community, are willing to work hand-in-hand to make it a better product. Suggestions are encouraged within the platforms so as to improve its capabilities and uses.

Taken together, these factors help instill confidence in the future of the currency.

Challenges facing Dash

The branding of Dash somewhat presents a barrier to trading and/or its widespread market adoption. Most traders are wary about it and are less inclined to accept it, due to the fact that it was initially associated with illegal activities of the dark web, as mentioned in the beginning. This resulted in the Dash brand ending up in more of a niche market rather than in the mainstream.

There have been concerns that the use of Masternodes could make it an easy target for hackers and that this would paralyze the cryptocurrency in a way no one can predict. So far, this has not happened, but the possibility does exist. Similarly, there are reservations in many circles that the proposed technological innovations around the currency are not necessarily an innovation but a mere improvement on the existing ideas of cryptocurrencies, and so one should not judge its potential on that point alone. The product and its benefits definitely should be tested by more people and should provide more transparency regarding the quality of the testing procedures, if they want to alleviate fears.

Dash is not as popular as its other counterparts, and the volume of trade is definitely lower. Its technology is also a bit new to most cryptocurrency investors. This makes it difficult to predict its possible trajectory or future outlook.

Is there a risk of Dash collapsing?

Rather than being a reason to celebrate, the sudden rise of Dash to such prominence among other cryptocurrencies has instead made investors a bit skeptical in trading the currency. I guess it's all about "If it sounds too good to be true …" Critics point out that this sudden rise might just be hype, and even though it may not crash immediately it will sooner or later come tumbling down. Whether or not this is true remains to be seen.

Unlike most cryptocurrencies, Dash is centrally controlled. This simply means that the developers control the governance systems and use the Masternodes to vote their own projects. This may make them act in their own interests and overlook the future of the currency.

Another aspect is that the amount of Dash being traded has not significantly changed, and it remains between 1,500-2,500. The pattern of exchange is generally flat although its value increases. Essentially depicting the *movement* of Dash rather than new *investments* in Dash.

The long and short of it is that it's hard to point out any clear indicators demonstrating an eminent crash in Dash. It is still a new currency and its trend in the market has not been monitored over a significant enough period of time to make educated assumptions. So the jury is still out on whether it will crash and burn or survive and thrive as a cryptocurrency.

References

Dash (2015, 3 April). 'DarkCoin is now Dash.' Retrieved from https://www.dash.org/

Dashtalk (2016, 15 June). 'Self-sustainable Decentralized Governance by blockchain.' Retrieved from https://dashtalk.org/

Eobot. 'What is Dash and Dash mining.' Retrieved from https://www.eobot.com/

Fintech. 'Dash: a superior digital money alternative to Bitcoin.' Retrived from http://www.fintech.finance/01-news/dash-a-superior-digital-money-alternative-to-bitcoin/

Fintekneeks.'Decentralized retirement plan.' Retrieved from https://steemit.com/

Higgins, S. (2017, 2 March). The $45-Dollar Question: What's Going On With the Price of Dash? Retrieved from https://www.coindesk.com/the-45-dollar-question-dash-whats-going-on/

Kharif, O. (2017, 8 March). Investors Who Missed Bitcoin Rally Go for Dash, Ether, Monero. Retrieved from https://www.bloomberg.com/news/articles/2017-03-08/investors-who-missed-bitcoin-rally-go-for-dash-Ether-monero

Memoria, F. (May 2017). 'Dash enters the Billion Dollar Cryptocurrency Club.' Retrieved from https://cryptocoinsnews.com/

Reddit. 'Dash is digital currency.' Retrieved from https/www.reddit.com/

Chapter 8: Conclusion

Cryptocurrencies have made significant gains in the last decade. While their beginnings may not have been especially encouraging, it is clear that their future is something to be taken seriously. The question is, should you join the train now, or wait until they become legally mandated mediums of exchange and have completely replaced money as we know it today?

Despite initial resistance for many quarters, cryptocurrencies, particularly Bitcoin, have emerged not only as alternative means of payment, but the technology behind them is being harnessed for use in many different ways. Blockchain technologies and Smart Contracts t are facilitating all kinds of transactions. Fund transfers have been made easier, faster, and cheaper whereby institutions that would traditionally see these technologies as rivals are adopting them. Prediction markets have been energised and the banking industry now considers Ripple more as a tool than a rival to the sector.

Though there remain reservations about one of the most basic elements of cryptocurrencies – the absence of State regulation – many in the financial and business worlds see these digital currencies as the 'currency of the future.' This view is shared by many individual and institutional investors as well as financial analysts.

I have laid bare what these digital currencies bring to the table and what their current (and potential) challenges are. It is obvious that cryptocurrencies have the potential to change the global economic landscape, and despite the challenges attached to them, many indicators point toward the widespread adoption of the blockchain technology in the future.

So, should you jump in at the deep end and invest in cryptocurrencies immediately? Should you wait and see how things go? with additional research and advice However, if in fact you do decide to get involved, how should you go about it? This last question is relatively easy to answer as I have provided you with a wealth of information on the different ways to invest in cryptocurrencies..

It is true that everybody has a different risk threshold, but for most people, information is the critical factor that determines whether a decision is an informed risk or a reckless one. I hope that the information I have provided to you in this book will jumpstart your inquiry and enable you to have meaningful discussions. Discussions that will hopefully lead you to the path of financial success in the years ahead.

www.ingramcontent.com/pod-product-compliance
Lightning Source LLC
LaVergne TN
LVHW041640060526
838200LV00040B/1647